SAVOR
San Francisco

RECIPES FROM SAN FRANCISCO'S TOP RESTAURANTS
WITH WINES FROM CALIFORNIA'S BEST WINERIES

ELIZABETH ALAIN

Featuring food photography by Kate Baldwin

Cover design by Jeanne Hendrickson, Hendrickson Design
Text design & layout by Jeanne Hendrickson, Hendrickson Design

Published by Sea Script Company
Seattle, Washington

ISBN: 0-9672186-8-3
Library of Congress Card Catalog Number: 2005931705
08 07 06 05 04   1 2 3 4 5

Printed in Hong Kong
Magnum Printing

Books can be purchased through: www.savorseries.com
Other Savor Series books released/due for release:
Savor Seattle (2005)
Savor Las Vegas
Savor Mexico
Savor Montreal
Savor New Orleans
Savor Beijing

Sea Script
SEA SCRIPT COMPANY
1800 westlake ave n. ste 205 seattle wa 98109
tel 206.748.0345 fax 206.748.0343
www.savorseries.com

CONTENTS

Few cities evoke the emotional response and visual images that San Francisco does. It's a place of dreams. With an historical lexicon that includes Barbary Coast, California Gold Rush, Golden Gate Bridge, Haight–Ashbury, Financial Center of the West, Ghirardelli Chocolate, the Giants and the 49ers, it's no wonder so many hearts have been left (or found) in San Francisco.

Topping the list of San Francisco attractions is its cornucopia of fine dining. Its restaurants range from fresh California, French, Chinese, and Italian to Vietnamese, Greek, Polynesian and everything in–between— each representing the strong cultural influences in this international city. Pair the extraordinary food with the world–class wines of California's wine country and you have an epicurean and wine lover's paradise.

Within the forty–nine square miles of the city, you can enjoy fine dining before or after seeing the sights strolling along Fisherman's Wharf, Chinatown, the Presidio, Union Square, the Embarcadero; or climbing San Francisco's 'hills' – Nob Hill, Russian Hill, Potrero Hill; or taking in a game at SBC Park.

San Francisco. If you've been, you'll always remember it. If you haven't been, you'll want to go.

Savor San Francisco!

Publisher

Dedicated to Ann Forsyth

ALWAYS AN INSPIRATION

The restaurants and wineries

WHO AGREED TO SHARE THEIR BEST SO WE CAN ENJOY
THEIR BEST IN OUR HOMES

Jeanne Hendrickson

WHO BRINGS HER INCREDIBLE TALENTS AND STYLE
TO EVERY BOOK SHE TOUCHES

Jacqueline Curran

WHO OPENED THE DOORS AND INTRODUCED US TO
THESE 25 SUPERB RESTAURANTS

XII

Kylee Krida

WHO BROUGHT ORDER TO THE INFORMATION

Anina Layton

WHO LENT HER EYE TO THE WORDS

John and Kirstin, Jamie, Brooke and Colleen

WHO MAKE IT ALL A DELIGHT

Salmon Carpaccio with the Colors of Spring

Breast of Chicken Wrapped in Pancetta

Rabbit Ragu alla Cacciatora

Warm Zabaglione Scented with Orange–Muscat Liqueur

Acquerello

ACQUERELLO
GIANCARLO PATERLINI,
OWNER
SUZETTE GRESHAM,
OWNER

1722 SACRAMENTO STREET

SAN FRANCISCO, CA 94109

415.567.5432

WWW.ACQUERELLO.COM

ACQUERELLO MEANS "WATERCOLOR" IN ITALIAN, AND ENTERING THE restaurant's dining room is like stepping into a painting. Pale yellow walls and original watercolors of Venetian scenes and Palladian villas are softly illuminated with Murano lamps. Large bouquets of fresh flowers and a collection of crystal decanters softly blend color and light. The former chapel is graced with arches and a rustic wood–beamed ceiling.

Chef Suzette Gresham creatively reinvents traditional dishes from all regions of Italy in a lighter, more contemporary style. Herb Roasted Loin of Veal, deglazed with red wine in its own sauce of guanciale, porcini mushrooms and pearl onions and her Spicy Saffron Tagliolini "aglio e olio" with tuna and bottarga from Sardinia give testament to her culinary skill. Upon awarding her the Rachel H. Norman Award, the committee commented, "this was the first year of awarding to other than a chef of French cuisine."

Giancarlo Paterlini, a native of Bologna, is acclaimed and consulted as one of America's leading Italian wine experts. "Every aspiring sommelier in town should be required to study his elegant, informed approach." (*San Francisco* Magazine) His particular strengths lie in his talent for pairing foods with the ideal wines and in the impeccable European standard he brings to the seamless and elegant dining room service.

Hailed as number two on its list of America's ten best Italian restaurants, *Wine Spectator* bestowed the restaurant its coveted Award of Excellence. Acquerello recently celebrated its 15th year and ranks among the most romantic, best Italian and best splurge spots in San Francisco.

Salmon Carpaccio with the Colors of Spring

❖ SALMON   SERVES 6

12-16 OZ FRESH SALMON FILET,
CLEANED AND DEBONED
(REQUEST THICK FILETS FROM
NEAR THE SALMON HEAD)
1 ROLL PLASTIC WRAP
1 OZ EXTRA VIRGIN OLIVE OIL
KOSHER SALT
FRESH GROUND BLACK PEPPER
1/2 RED BELL PEPPER,
TINY DICE (BRUNOISE)
1/2 YELLOW BELL PEPPER, BRUNOISE
1 GREEN ZUCCHINI, SLICE 1/8" THICK
IN LENGTHWISE STRIPS
1/2 BUNCH CHIVES, BRUNOISE OR
DIAMOND SHAPE
1 LEMON, ZEST REMOVED,
WITHOUT PITH
2-3 TSP LEMON JUICE, STRAINED
1 HEAD BUTTER LETTUCE,
OUTER LEAVES REMOVED
2 TBSP CHIVE BLOSSOMS

❖ With a sharp knife, sculpt salmon into a round "log" shape. Remove silver or blood lines. Place the salmon on a piece of plastic wrap. Center on the edge closest to you. With slight tension, roll the salmon in the plastic wrap away from you. Grasp both ends of the plastic wrap and roll on the table, forcing the salmon to take on a cylindrical shape. Pinch the ends and tie into knots up close to the salmon. You should have a well-rounded "log" of salmon. Place in the freezer the night before or at least 4 hours before serving.

Remove the salmon from the freezer. Allow to temper for 15 minutes. Lightly brush the center of a flat surface serving plate with extra virgin olive oil. Thinly slice the salmon, 1/8" to 1/4" thick. Beginning with the outside perimeter of the plate, lay each slice down, slightly overlapping the previous slice. (Once defrosted, the fish is very soft.)

Continue to decoratively fill in the center of the plate until covered. Cover the salmon with plastic wrap making contact but do not pull taut. With a flat-sided meat pounder, evenly apply gentle pressure to the salmon. Leave the plastic wrap in place until you are ready to serve.

❖ LEMON EGG CREAM

5 EGG YOLKS, ROOM TEMPERATURE
3-5 GARLIC CLOVES,
PEELED AND CRACKED
2 LEMONS, SQUEEZED AND STRAINED
1/2 CUP EXTRA VIRGIN OLIVE OIL
1/2 CUP PURE OLIVE OIL
KOSHER SALT
GROUND WHITE PEPPER

❖ Using a stand mixer with the paddle attachment, slowly mix the egg yolks and garlic cloves. Drizzle in a little lemon juice to thin out the yolks. Sprinkle in a little salt and pepper. Drizzle 1/4 of one of the olive oils in a thin continuous stream. Do the same with the other olive oil. Do not feed in the oil faster than the eggs can take it without breaking up. Scrape down the sides of the bowl with a rubber spatula. Alternate the lemon juice, seasonings and olive oil until desired thickness and flavor. Load the mixture into a squirt bottle with a tip. Set aside.

❖ LEMON VINAIGRETTE

3-4 TBSP EXTRA VIRGIN OLIVE OIL
1 LEMON, JUICED
SALT AND PEPPER TO TASTE

❖ Place lemon juice in a small bowl. Using a whisk, drizzle in extra virgin olive oil to taste. Add a pinch of salt and white pepper.

Quickly blanch the dices of the red and yellow bell peppers and the zucchini. Drain and dry on paper towels. Set aside. With a sharp knife, cut superfine julienne of lemon zest. Set aside. Cut little tiny chives, set aside.

ASSEMBLY

Remove the salmon from the refrigerator. Remove the plastic wrap. Brush the salmon with olive oil. Season with salt and ground pepper. Apply a design on the salmon with the Lemon Egg Cream. Lightly scatter lemon zest, bell pepper pieces, and the zucchini pieces on top. Sprinkle with chives and chive blossoms.

In a small bowl, drizzle the Lemon Vinaigrette over the torn pieces of butter lettuce. Season with salt and pepper. Center a little stack of lettuce leaves on top of the salmon. Serve immediately. Buon Appetito!

Breast of Chicken Wrapped in Pancetta

SERVES 4

Remove visual fat or tendons from the breasts. Lightly rub a small amount of minced garlic over the breasts. Place one large sage leaf on top of each breast.

Starting with the underside of the chicken breast, snugly wrap 1 slice of pancetta around one end of the breast. Continue to wrap the remaining 3 slices around the length of the breast. Allow each layer to slightly overlap the previous layer. Continue until the entire breast is covered. Use a toothpick to tuck the loose end under the last 2 wraps to anchor the pancetta.

Heat a flat pan over medium high heat. Add the olive oil. Place the wrapped breasts onto the pan, one at a time. Lightly brown on all sides. (Don't let the pancetta get crisp or hard.) Remove the chicken from the pan. Set aside.

❖ Deglaze the pan with the brandy, cooking briefly. Whisk to loosen the pan drippings. Whisk in the chicken stock. Reduce a little. Add the poultry demi glaze. Season to taste with salt and pepper. Cook until slightly thickened. Strain and set aside.

ASSEMBLY

Place seared chicken on a cooking tray. Finish in the oven until just done. Remove and let rest. Arrange a selection of seasonal vegetables on a preheated serving plate. At a slight diagonal, slice the wrapped chicken with a sharp knife. Keep slices in order. Fan out the chicken slices, leaning them against the vegetables. Drizzle the Brandy Sauce around the perimeter. Garnish with a sage sprig. Serve immediately.

4 6 OZ CHICKEN BREASTS, SKINLESS
1/2 TSP GARLIC, MINCED
4 SAGE LEAVES, LARGE, NO STEMS
16 PANCETTA SLICES, THIN AND CIRCULAR (4 SLICES PER BREAST)
1 TSP OLIVE OIL
4 SAGE SPRIGS FOR GARNISH

5

❖ BRANDY SAUCE
2 OZ BRANDY
4 OZ CHICKEN STOCK
3-4 OZ POULTRY DEMI GLAZE
KOSHER SALT
FRESH GROUND WHITE PEPPER

Rabbit Ragu alla Cacciatora

3 WHOLE RABBITS
2 CUPS WHITE WINE
2 CUPS CHICKEN OR RABBIT STOCK
1 STALK CELERY, CUT IN CHUNKS
1 YELLOW OINION, CUT IN CHUNKS
1 CARROT, CUT IN CHUNKS
3 SPRIGS THYME
3 CUPS YELLOW ONION, DICED
1/2 CUP SHALLOTS, DICED
6 CLOVES GARLIC, MINCED
1/4 CUP THYME, MINCED
1/4 CUP SAGE, MINCED
1 TBSP ROSEMARY, MINCED
1/4 CUP PARSLEY, MINCED
EXTRA VIRGIN OLIVE OIL
2 CUPS WHITE WINE
4 CUPS RED WINE
2 CUPS DRIED PORCINI MUSHROOMS
1 LB FRESH CHANTERELLE MUSHROOMS
1 LB FRESH SHIITAKE MUSHROOMS
1 QT RABBIT STOCK
6 TOMATOES, BLANCHED, PEELED, AND DICED
SALT AND PEPPER

SERVES 6

This ragu is a flavorful rendition of the classic "hunter's style" sauce, using rabbit instead of poultry. We are serving this ragu tossed with wide pappardelle noodles.

Season the whole rabbit with salt and pepper. Lightly sear in a heavy skillet. Deglaze with 1 cup white wine and 2 cups of rabbit or chicken stock. Add chunks of celery, onion, carrot and the thyme sprigs. Cover with a tight fitting lid. Braise at 350° for approximately 15 to 20 minutes until meat is just set. Allow to rest in the liquid to finish. Cool.

Remove rabbit meat from bones in large pieces, avoiding cartilage and sinew. Reserve stock. Cut into 2" by 1/2" pieces. In a large flat bottom Rondeau, sweat diced onion, shallot, garlic and herbs in olive oil until soft. Add red wine and simmer until almost reduced by half. Soak porcini mushrooms in hot water until soft. Remove and rough chop. Drain through fine strainer. Add to wine reduction.

In a separate sauté pan, sweat fresh mushrooms seasoned with whole garlic and thyme. Splash with white wine and braise until tender. Add braised mushrooms, strained porcini liquid, tomatoes and the stock from the wine reduction. Cook ragu until flavorful, fortifying with veal glaze and tomato purée if needed. Add rabbit meat. Simmer to warm through. Adjust seasonings. Do not overcook rabbit.

Warm Zabaglione Scented with Orange-Muscat Liqueur

SERVES 4–6

4 EGG YOLKS

1/8 CUP MOSCATO DI PANTELLERIA

OR TRIPLE SEC

1/4 CUP WHITE WINE

1 1/2 TBSP GRANULATED SUGAR

2 TBSP AMARETTI COOKIE CRUMBS

2 ORANGES, PEELED AND

SLICED IN SECTIONS

Traditional Zabaglione is made with Marsala wine. Our variation of this classic dessert is made with Moscato di Pantelleria, an elegant after-dinner wine of Muscat grapes imported from Italy. If Moscato di Pantelleria is not available, simply substitute Triple Sec.

Prepare tall martini glasses by adding 1 tbsp of the Amaretti crumbs at the bottom. Top with a few of the orange sections. Drizzle with a little of the juice.

In a copper or stainless steel bowl, combine the egg yolks with all of the liquid ingredients and sugar. Whisk until fully incorporated. Place bowl over a simmering water bath. Whisk continuously and rapidly. Be careful not to let the eggs coagulate on the sides of the bowl. Whisk until well thickened and holds a ribbon when the whisk is lifted above the bowl. Spoon Zabaglione on top of the oranges and Amaretti crumbs. Garnish with Candied Orange Peel.

❖ CANDIED ORANGE PEEL

2 ORANGES

1 CUP WATER

1 CUP SUGAR

GRANULATED SUGAR

❖ Julienne zest from oranges. Avoid the pith. Bring water and sugar to a boil forming a simple syrup. Add the orange zest. Simmer for 15 minutes or until there is very little bitterness. Remove zest from syrup and drain. Place zest on a layer of granulated sugar and sprinkle more sugar on top to coat the orange zest and orange peel. Let cool. Store in an airtight container.

Wine Pairing

SALMON CARPACCIO WITH THE COLORS OF SPRING
JORDAN 2003 RUSSIAN RIVER VALLEY CHARDONNAY

BREAST OF CHICKEN WRAPPED IN PANCETTA
JORDAN 2003 RUSSIAN RIVER VALLEY CHARDONNAY

RABBIT RAGU' ALLA CACCIATORE
JORDAN 2001 SONOMA COUNTY CABERNET SAUVIGNON

WARM ZABGLIONE SECENTED WITH ORANGE–MUSCAT LIQUEUR
JORDAN 1999 SONOMA COUNTY CABERNET SAUVIGNON

8

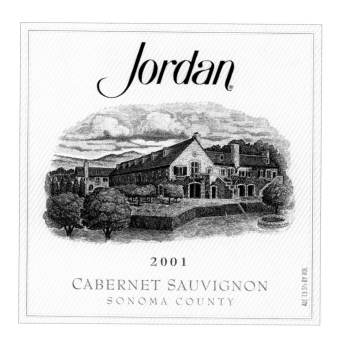

2001

CABERNET SAUVIGNON
SONOMA COUNTY

ALC 13.5% BY VOL

JORDAN VINEYARD
& WINERY

TOM JORDAN,
OWNER

1474 ALEXANDER VALLEY ROAD

HEALDSBURG, CA 95448

800.654.1213

WWW.JORDANWINERY.COM

IN 1972, TOM JORDAN ACQUIRED 275 ACRES OF PRUNE ORCHARDS IN the Alexander Valley for conversion to vineyards. He also purchased 1300 acres of rolling oak woodlands as a site for the future winery facility and as an informal preserve for deer, wild turkey, coyotes, waterfowl and other wildlife.

In the areas selected for planting vines, nature required the help of art and experience so the land was regraded to enhance soil drainage. Cabernet Sauvignon, Merlot and, five years later, Chardonnay grapes were planted. In due course, a winery inspired by French country architecture was built on an oak-studded knoll and completed just in time for Jordan Winery's first vintage in 1976.

From the beginning, winemaking at Jordan has integrated new-world technology and old-world artistry to complement the unique natural qualities of the grapes. Created under the tutelage of the legendary André Tchelistcheff, the first vintage of Cabernet Sauvignon established a suppleness and delicacy that was uncommon in California. Working alongside André in those early years was the present winemaker, Rob Davis. Many of the vineyard workers who originally planted the estate vines still care for them today. This continuity ensures the consistency of style and elegance so typical of all Jordan wines.

Tom Jordan has always believed that winemaking should be a logical conclusion to the all-important work done in the vineyards. His instincts proved to be right. Jordan Winery quickly gained an international reputation for excellence and it continues to maintain its high quality in every bottle it produces.

GARLIC PRAWNS

QUAIL

SEARED MEKONG BASA

VIETNAMESE COFFEE POT DE CRÈME

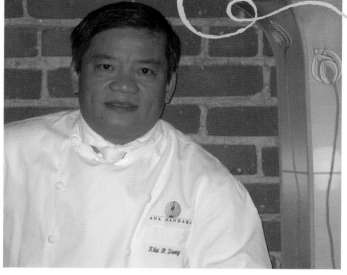

Ana Mandara
Khai Duong,
Executive Chef

891 beach street
san francisco, ca 94109
415.771.6800
www.anamandara.com

Ana Mandara, "beautiful refuge" in Vietnamese, is just that. Amidst the soft lighting, silken setting and the palm fronds, the intriguing mix of opulence and Asian simplicity welcomes you.

Designed by Aline Ho and Peter McKinley, the main dining area is a breathtaking space that is both elegant and casual. Architectural elements evoke Vietnam's rich cultural heritage, from the traditional to the colonial. The combination of level changes and subtle textiles results in an intimate ambiance that captures the romance of a bygone era while maintaining a freshness that is undeniably modern. Decorative accents including artifacts and antiques, intricate carvings, pottery, fountains and tropical foliage.

Classically trained Executive Chef Khai Duong is a native of Nha-Trang, Vietnam. As a summa cum laude graduate of Le Cordon Bleu Academie Culinaire de Paris, Chef Khai Duong's success comes from his ability to prepare Vietnamese recipes using French techniques with a dash of American style—Vegetarian Bo Bia with Julienne Vegetables and Tofu Wrapped with Fine Rice Paper; Banana Blossom Salad with Chicken and Grapefruit; Grilled Rack of Lamb with Vietnamese Cinnamon-Star Anise Rub and Spicy Tamarind Sauce; and Crispy Mango Springrolls with Coconut, Vanilla Crème Anglaise and Mango Sauce. Accompany your meal with wine from their discriminating wine list or tea from their own plantation.

"This is serious, sophisticated, expertly crafted food that seamlessly melds the refined yet exotic flavors of Vietnam with classic French culinary techniques and California's joyous spirit of food adventure." (*San Francisco Examiner*)

In Vietnamese culture, the crane and the turtle in Ana Mandara's logo symbolize enduring power and longevity. The two, standing together, represent a healthy and long life of happiness. This is Ana Mandara's wish for you when you visit the "beautiful refuge."

Garlic Prawns

1 LB WHITE PRAWNS, PEELED,
DEVEINED AND BUTTERFLIED
4 TBSP OLIVE OIL
1 BUNCH WATER SPINACH OR
ORDINARY SPINACH
OLIVE OIL

❖ Mix together prawns, garlic, black pepper, fish sauce, basil and olive oil. Transfer to bowl and refrigerate until ready to use.

❖ MARINADE
5 CLOVES GARLIC, MINCED
1/2 TSP FRESHLY GROUND BLACK PEPPER
2 TBSP THAI BASIL, FINELY CHOPPED
2 TBSP FISH SAUCE
3 TBSP OLIVE OIL

❖ In medium skillet, heat 4 tbsp olive oil over high heat until hot. Reduce to medium-high heat. Add remaining garlic, stirring for 30 seconds. Add chopped onion, stirring for another 30 seconds. Deglaze with rice wine. Add ground chili, tomatoes, sugar and 5 tbsp fish sauce. Let simmer, stirring occasionally until thickened. Remove sauce from heat and set aside.

❖ TOMATO SAUCE
2 LB FRESH TOMATOES, PEELED,
SEEDED AND CHOPPED
4 TBSP OLIVE OIL
3 OZ CHINESE RICE WINE
(NOT RICE WINE VINEGAR)
1/2 TSP GROUND CHILI
1/2 MEDIUM WHITE ONION,
FINELY CHOPPED
1 TBSP SUGAR
5 TBSP FISH SAUCE

❖ Cook spinach noodles in a large pot of boiling water with salt and 1 tbsp vegetable oil. Stir occasionally until firm but tender. Pour off hot water. Refill pot with warm water. Drain and repeat. Drain well, tossing noodles often. In large skillet over medium-high heat, heat 1/4" of vegetable oil. Start shaping the Galette by pressing 1/4 lb of noodles into the palm of your hand creating a circular flat form, 2" wide. Place noodle Galette in hot oil and fry until brown and crisp on both sides. Be sure to turn over Galette as needed when frying. Remove and place on paper towel to absorb excess oil.

❖ NOODLE GALETTE
1 LB CHINESE SPINACH NOODLES
2 TBSP VEGETABLE OIL
1/2 TSP SALT

In a large skillet, heat 4 tbsp olive oil over medium-high heat until hot. Place prawns in oil and cook until medium. Remove prawns and set aside. Place skillet back on stove with a small amount of oil to quickly wilt the water spinach.

ASSEMBLY

Using dinner plates, put 4 full tbsp of tomato sauce in center. Place noodle Galette on top. Arrange 4 prawns on top of the Galette with tails directed away from center. Place the sautéed water spinach on top of the prawns for a final touch.

Quail

QUAIL

4 BONELESS QUAIL

1 TBSP SALT

1 TBSP GROUND BLACK PEPPER

2 TBSP CANOLA OIL

Towel dry quail. Season with salt and pepper outside as well as in the cavity. Sear the quail until golden brown in a sauté pan, breast side down. Turn over and place in oven at 350° for 10 minutes.

PRUNE SAUCE

5 DRIED PRESERVED PRUNES

1 TBSP VEGETABLE OIL

1 CLOVE GARLIC, MINCED

PINCH DRIED CHILI FLAKES

1/4 CUP HOISIN SAUCE

1 TSP CREAMY PEANUT BUTTER

1 TBSP CORN STARCH

1 TBSP WATER

In a small saucepan, cover the prunes with 2 cups water. Bring to a boil over high heat, reduce to low and simmer until the prunes are soft, about 8 minutes. Reserving the water, remove the prunes with a slotted spoon and pit them. Chop the prunes finely and set aside.

In a small saucepan, heat the oil over medium heat. Add the garlic, prunes and chili flakes. Cook, stirring, for 1 minute. Add the reserved prune water, hoisin sauce and peanut butter. Simmer for 1 minute. Mix the cornstarch with the 1 tbsp water. Stir into the sauce. Simmer, stirring, until thickened and smooth, about 1 minute. Serve hot or at room temperature.

STICKY RICE

2 CUPS STICKY RICE OR

BLACK SWEET RICE

2 1/2 CUPS WATER

1 CUP SHIITAKE MUSHROOMS

3 TBSP SHALLOTS, CHOPPED

1 TBSP FISH SAUCE

2 TBSP CANOLA OIL

1 TBSP BUTTER

Sauté shiitake mushrooms and shallots until golden brown with canola oil, finish with butter and fish sauce. Reserve. After cooking rice, add the mushroom mixture to the rice.

13

Seared Mekong Basa

4 7 OZ FILETS OF BASA
OR DOVER SOLE
1 CUP FLOUR
SALT AND BLACK PEPPER

SERVES 4

Season the filet with salt and black pepper. Dust filet lightly with flour, shaking off excess flour. Heat oil in a medium size sauté pan until hot. Add Basa filet to hot sauté pan, reducing heat slightly. Cook until golden brown on both sides, approximately 3 minutes per side.

❖ SAUCE

1 TBSP OF CHILI SAUCE
1 TBSP OF WHITE VINEGAR
1/2 CUP OF FISH SAUCE (NUOC MAM)
1/4 CUP OF FRESH LIME JUICE
1/2 CUP SUGAR
3 TBSP OF RICE FLOUR
(WITH 3 TBSP OF WATER TO
DISSOLVE THE RICE FLOUR)

❖ Combine all sauce ingredients except the rice flour in a medium size sauté pan. Bring to boil. Combine rice flour and water in bowl, stirring to make a smooth mixture. Slowly add water-flour mixture to the boiling sauce until it is a creamy consistency. Adjust seasoning and reserve.

❖ PEA SPROUTS

2 CLOVES GARLIC, CHOPPED
1/2 LB SNOW PEA SPROUTS
OLIVE OIL FOR SAUTÉ

❖ Add oil to sauté pan and place over moderate heat. Add chopped garlic and sauté until fragrant. Add pea sprouts and quickly stir-fry, being careful not to burn garlic.

14

❖ CILANTRO OIL GARNISH

1 BUNCH CILANTRO
1/4 CUP OLIVE OIL

❖ Marinate cilantro in olive oil overnight. In a blender, pulse cilantro and olive oil to a smooth purée. Pass through a fine sieve. Reserve for garnish.

ASSEMBLY

Place pea sprouts in center of plate. Place Basa filet on pea sprouts. Top with sauce and cilantro oil.

Vietnamese Coffee Pot de Crème

SERVES 4

2 CUPS CREAM
1/2 VANILLA BEAN
6 EGG YOLKS
1/2 CUPS SUGAR
1/8 TSP SALT
1 1/2 TSP VIETNAMESE COFFEE GROUNDS
1 CUP WHIPPED CREAM FOR TOPPING
MINT SPRIGS FOR GARNISH

Preheat oven to 350°.

Heat 1 3/4 cups of cream, the vanilla bean and the coffee grounds in saucepan over medium heat.

In a small bowl, beat egg yolks until light and lemon colored. Gradually beat in sugar and salt plus the remaining 1/4 cup of cream. Slowly beat in the hot coffee cream mixture.

Strain coffee mixture into cream pots or custard cups. Place them in a baking pan and pour in hot water to 1" depth. Cover pots with foil. Bake in a preheated oven 20 to 25 minutes or until a knife inserted in the center comes out clean. Cool and chill before serving. Serve in a martini glass. Garnish with whipped cream and a sprig of mint.

15

Wine Pairing

16

GARLIC PRAWNS
CARNEROS PINOT GRIS

QUAIL
CARNEROS PINOT NOIR

SEARED MEKONG BASA
CARNEROS HEIRLOOM PINOT NOIR

VIETNAMESE COFFEE POT DE CRÈME
NAPA VALLEY MERLOT

THIS WINE WAS CELLARED AND BOTTLED BY ETUDE WINES
RUTHERFORD, CALIFORNIA · ALCOHOL 13.5% BY VOLUME

ETUDE
WINES

BERINGER BLASS
WINE ESTATES,
OWNER

PO BOX 3382

NAPA, CA 94558

707.257.5300

WWW.ETUDEWINES.COM

ETUDE BEGAN AS A PHILOSOPHY NOT A PLACE, ALTHOUGH TONY SOTER dreamed of one day creating a perfect home for his wines. That dream became a reality with the acquisition of a winery in Carneros. Transformed into a state-of-the-art facility for producing world class Pinot Noir and Cabernet Sauvignon, the winery consists of three beautiful masonry buildings totaling 40,000 square feet that occupy a picturesque setting just a few miles from Etude's estate Carneros vineyard.

The winery is built in the French style amidst mature landscaping. Soter believes this is the ideal location because of its proximity to Etude's Carneros Pinot Noir sources and its easy accessibility to the upper Napa Valley Cabernet Sauvignon vineyards.

Though modeled on the best from Burgundy and Bordeaux, Etude's Pinot Noir and Cabernet Sauvignon speak clearly of their contemporary California origins, combining rich, ripe fruit with an elegant structure and opulent mouthfeel. Etude's Pinot Noirs, including a highly esteemed bottling made from rare heirloom varieties, and its small production of Pinot Gris and Pinot Blanc are vinified from grapes grown in the cool Carneros region. Fruit for the winery's Cabernet Sauvignon and Merlot is sourced from the warmer northern half of Napa Valley.

The high quality of the grapes Etude grows and sources, combined with the skill and experience of Tony Soter, explain why Etude wines consistently earn the highest accolades from consumers, the trade and wine critics. "I like to challenge wine mythology and conventional wisdom while playing homage to the classical standards. It's my effort to better understand and execute the craft of traditional winegrowing." - Tony Soter

PISTACHIO CRUSTED GOAT CHEESE WITH ONION–RAISIN JAM

FRESH FAVA BEAN, ASPARAGUS AND PEA SALAD

SLOW BRAISED BEEF SHORTRIBS WITH CELERY AND HERB SALAD

CRÈME CARAMEL WITH EAU DE ROSE

Baraka

BARAKA
RICHARD TERZAGHI,
EXECUTIVE CHEF
DAVID BAZIRGAN,
EXECUTIVE CHEF
DARREN PRESS,
PATISSIER

288 CONNECTICUT STREET
SAN FRANCISCO, CA 94107
415.255.0387
WWW.BARAKASF.NET

IN MANY CULTURES BARAKA IS COMMONLY USED AS A BLESSING. Enter the world of Baraka restaurant through its velvet curtain and you discover the blessings of French Mediterranean fare by Executive Chef David Bazirgan, nominated one of 2005's top five rising chefs of San Francisco. The burnt orange colored walls, copper tabletops, velvet cushioned banquettes, warmly lit by soft lighting, set the mood for what's to come. The engaging Mediterranean décor amply complements the restaurant's cuisine.

French owners Jocelyn Bulow, and Karine and Richard Terzaghi bring what they know best to this Potrero Hill nightspot—good food served by a knowledgeable and friendly staff.

Sip on a Rose Water Sakitini or rose wine with rose petals as you savor the sweet and salty flavor of the Stuffed Dates with Chorizo, Cabrales, Jamon Serrano and Frisee Salad, the Moroccan-style Meatballs with Goat Yogurt Fomage Blanc, the Seafood Paella with fresh local fish, and the Cinnamon Scented Couscous with Pistachio and Golden Raisins. Be sure to order the grilled flatbread with zahatar to scoop up every last bit of the Paella.

When it's busy in the restaurant, you can lounge on the couches in Baraka's cozy private room and be served the same menu as the main dining room.

"Baraka is at the top of its game, continually evolving to keep the concept fresh and to ensure that customers will return month after month." (*San Francisco Chronicle*)

Pistachio Crusted Goat Cheese with Onion-Raisin Jam

❖ ONION-RAISIN JAM

2 LARGE YELLOW ONIONS, SLICED THIN

2 TBSP GRAPE SEED OIL

1 TBSP CHOPPED THYME

1 TSP RAS AL HANOUT (MOROCCAN FOR A BLEND OF CUMIN, GINGER, PAPRIKA, CINNAMON AND SAFFRON)

3 TBSP SUGAR

1/2 CUP GOLDEN RAISINS PLUMPED IN WARM WATER

SALT AND PEPPER TO TASTE

❖ PISTACHIO CRUSTED GOAT CHEESE

4 2 OZ BALLS YOUNG GOAT CHEESE

1 CUP ALL PURPOSE FLOUR

2 EGGS, BEATEN

1 CUP PISTACHIOS, TOASTED AND COARSELY GROUND

1/2 CUP WARM HONEY

SERVES 4

❖ In a large saucepan, heat the oil on low. Add the onions and a pinch of salt. Cook covered for 1 hour, stirring occasionally. When very soft, add the remaining ingredients. Cook for an additional 5 minutes. Season to taste with salt and pepper. Allow to cool to room temperature.

❖ Preheat oven to 350°.

Form the goat cheese balls into 1" thick patties. Use three small bowls: one for flour, one for the eggs, one for the pistachios. First, dust the patties in the flour. Pat off any excess flour. Dip the floured patties lightly into the egg mixture, just enough to coat. Lastly, roll the patties in the pistachios, evenly coating the whole goat cheese patty.

Place the goat cheese on a cookie sheet. Place in the oven for about 6 minutes, until just warm through.

ASSEMBLY

Place a small mound of the onion jam in the center of 4 room temperature plates. Using a spatula, place the goat cheese on each of the mounds. Drizzle with honey.

Fresh Fava Bean, Asparagus and Pea Salad

2 CUPS FRESH FAVA BEANS, BLANCHED AND SHELLED

1 BUNCH THIN ASPARAGUS, PEELED, BLANCHED AND CUT INTO 1 1/2" PIECES

2 CUPS FRESH PEAS, SHELLED AND BLANCHED

1 TBSP CILANTRO, CHOPPED

1 TBSP MINT, CHOPPED

❖ VINAIGRETTE

1 TSP GARLIC, MINCED

2 TBSP LEMON JUICE

1 TSP GROUND CUMIN

2 TSP GROUND MILD PAPRIKA

1 CUP EXTRA VIRGIN OLIVE OIL

SALT AND PEPPER

SERVES 4

❖ Mix all ingredients well with a whisk.

ASSEMBLY

Mix the vegetables with the herbs and vinaigrette. Season to taste with salt and pepper. Distribute evenly among 4 chilled bowls. May also be served as an appetizer.

Slow Braised Beef Shortribs with Celery and Herb Salad

Allow 2 days to prepare.
Day 1 prep time: 1 hour to prep and 3 to 4 hours cooking time
Day 2 prep time: 1 hour and 20 minutes to reheat the ribs in the sauce

SERVES 4

EQUIPMENT NEEDED

LARGE CAST IRON SKILLET OR
HEAVY BOTTOM SAUTÉ PAN
TONGS
BRAISING PAN OR
ANY OVEN-SAFE METAL PAN
LARGE ENOUGH TO FIT THE RIBS,
SAUCE AND VEGGIES
ALUMINUM FOIL
SAUCEPAN

 ❖ SHORTRIBS

5 LB BONE-IN-BEEF SHORTRIBS
1 ONION, MEDIUM DICE
2 STALKS CELERY, MEDIUM DICE
2 CARROTS, MEDIUM DICE
2 CUPS RED WINE
1/2 CUP RED WINE VINEGAR
2 TBSP TOMATO PASTE
2 QT VEAL STOCK OR STORE-BOUGHT
DEMI-GLACE DILUTED WITH WATER
1 CINNAMON STICK
2 BAY LEAVES
5 SPRIGS OF FRESH THYME
5 STAR ANISE
1/2 TSP GROUND ALLSPICE
1 TSP GROUND CUMIN
SALT AND PEPPER TO TASTE
OLIVE OIL AS NEEDED

❖ Preheat oven to 325° convection or 350° non-convection. Season the ribs generously with salt and pepper on both sides.

Day 1

Heat the cast iron or sauté pan with 3 tbsp olive oil on medium-high heat. Place the ribs meat side down and cook for about 5 minutes until nicely browned but not burnt. Use the tongs to control the ribs. Turn over and cook the bone side for an additional 3 minutes.

Turn the heat to medium. Transfer the ribs to the braising pan, bone side down. Add the vegetables to the pan. Sauté for about 8 minutes until they begin to caramelize. Add the wine, red wine vinegar, tomato paste, herbs and spices. Stir well. Reduce until the mixture begins to thicken, about 3 minutes. Add the veal stock. Turn the heat to high. When it boils, shut the heat off. Pour the whole mixture over the ribs. Cover with aluminum foil and cook for 3 hours or until the ribs can be pierced by a knife with no resistance. The ribs should be very tender. Oven temperatures may vary, so more cooking time may be necessary.

Remove the ribs. While still hot, use the tongs and a fork to remove the bones and discard. Strain the sauce. Set aside. (This recipe works best if you cool the ribs, refrigerate overnight and chill the sauce. This allows the ribs to be trimmed of fat and portioned, which is easier to do because, when cold, the fat will surface on the sauce and can be easily removed.)

❧ CELERY AND
HERB SALAD
1 CUP PARSLEY LEAVES
1/2 CUP CHIVES, 1" SNIPS
1/2 CUP TARRAGON LEAVES
3 CUPS CELERY, SLICED ON THE BIAS
ABOUT 1/8" THICK
1/2 CUP EXTRA VIRGIN OLIVE OIL
JUICE OF ONE MEYER LEMON
SALT AND PEPPER TO TASTE

Trim the ribs of fat. Cut into 6 to 8 nice portions. Take the top layer of fat off the sauce. Heat over medium heat in a saucepot large enough to hold the ribs and the sauce in one layer. When the sauce begins to simmer, add the ribs to the pot. Cover and simmer over low heat, 15 to 20 minutes until the ribs are very tender and hot throughout. Turn off burner and keep covered. While the ribs are heating, prepare the celery and herb salad.

❧ Combine all ingredients about 5 minutes before serving. (Any longer and the herbs will wilt.) Serve the ribs on warm plates. Serve with the salad.

This dish is great with glazed pearl onions, roasted sweet potatoes, mushrooms or any combination of the three.

Crème Caramel with Eau de Rose

❧ CARAMEL
2 CUPS SUGAR
1 CUP HOT WATER
PINCH OF CREAM OF TARTAR
(OR SUBSTITUTE WITH A FEW DROPS
OF LEMON JUICE OR WHITE VINEGAR)
8 EDIBLE ROSE PETALS

SERVES 4 TO 6

❧ Preheat oven to 350°.

Combine above ingredients in a heavy-bottom saucepot. Stir to make a paste. Place the pot on a high heat stovetop. Cook sugar until it turns an amber color, 4 to 8 minutes. Do not allow the sugar to become too dark and burn. Pour amber-colored sugar into a room temperature pot. Be careful! The sugar is very hot.

❧ CRÈME
4 CUPS MILK
1/4 VANILLA BEAN, SPLIT
4 WHOLE EGGS
4 YOLKS
1/2 CUP SUGAR
PINCH OF SALT
2 TBSP ROSE WATER

Lightly grease 4 to 6 6 oz ramekins. Warm in a 2" to 3" ovenproof baking dish. Pour a small amount of hot sugar into each ramekin. Pour excess molten sugar back into saucepot. (The goal is to have a thin coating of amber sugar in the bottom of each ramekin.) Set aside and let cool.

❧ Combine milk and vanilla in a medium size pot. Bring to a boil. Be careful not to boil over. Immediately remove from heat and set aside.

Combine eggs, yolks, sugar and salt in a bowl. Whisk together until well combined, forming a smooth, pale yellow paste. Using a ladle, very slowly add hot milk, gently whisking until egg mixture is tempered and milk is completely incorporated. Add rose water and gently stir. Pour mixed ingredients through a fine sieve. Let custard batter rest for 1 to 2 minutes. Skim off bubbles with ladle. Fill caramel ramekins with batter until almost full.

With ramekins in baking dish, surround with hot tap water until they are 3/4 submerged. Wave a blowtorch across the batter until small bubbles appear on the smooth surface (optional). Cover with aluminum foil. Poke 10 to 20 holes in top of foil creating steam vents. Gently place on middle rack in preheated 350° oven for approximately 45 to 75 minutes. Check often. Cook custard until set (just giggly in the center, jelly-like consistency). Remove from oven and let cool.

Remove ramekins from baking dish. Place in refrigerator for at least 1 hour. Cover each ramekin with plastic wrap. Refrigerate overnight.

ASSEMBLY

Run knife around edge of custard. Invert on cool plates. Remove ramekins and drain excess juices onto custard. Place one rose petal directly on top of each custard. Sprinkle "chiffonade" of rose petals around custards. Serve immediately.

Pistachio Crusted Goat Cheese with Onion–Raisin Jam
2002 Pazzo Proprietary Red

Fresh Fava Bean, Asparagus and Pea Salad
2000 Pazzo Proprietary Red

Slow Braised Beef Shortribs with Celery and Herb Salad
2002 Bacio Divino Proprietary Red

Crème Caramel with Eau de Rose
2001 Bacio Divino Proprietary Red

24

BACIO DIVINO
CELLARS

CLAUS JANZEN,
OWNER

PO BOX 131

RUTHERFORD, CA 94573

707.942.8101

WWW.BACIODIVINO.COM

OUR SMALL, FAMILY-RUN WINERY IS LOCATED IN THE HEART OF NAPA Valley. Since we began our wine program in 1993, we have maintained a single objective—to produce distinctive wines that encompass both terroir and human individuality.

At Bacio Divino, we make two proprietary blends. Our primary wine label, Bacio Divino, showcases the elegance and sophistication of Cabernet Sauvignon, with Sangiovese and Petit Sirah playing key supporting roles. Bacio Divino is a full-bodied wine, rich in black fruit flavors. This wine has always been enthusiastically received by wine critics.

More recently we've introduced Pazzo in which Sangiovese takes the starring role, supported by judicious proportions of Cabernet and Petit Sirah. Once again, our efforts were rewarded with favorable reviews. Intended to be a food-friendly wine, Pazzo offers abundant cherry overtones in the nose and palate.

No hard and fast "formula" governs either blend, however. Bacio Divino and Pazzo are, in the end, expressions of the land, the seasons that produce each vintage and expressions of the winemaker's personality.

Seared Diver Scallops, Celeriac Purée, Black Trumpets with Sauce Vermeer

Roasted Beet and Asian Pear Salad

Petite Angus Filet, Exotic Mushroom Mousse, Checkered Potato Salad
and Roasted Shallot Confit with Port Wine Reduction

Citrus Chocolate Cake

Citrus

CITRUS IN HOTEL VALENCIA
ON SANTANA ROW
PAUL ROHADFOX,
EXECUTIVE CHEF

355 SANTANA ROW
SAN JOSE, CA 95128
408.551.0010
WWW.HOTELVALENCIA.COM

CITRUS IS LOCATED IN HOTEL VALENCIA IN THE HEART OF SAN JOSE'S Santana Row, a European-inspired neighborhood of shops and haute couture boutiques that include Gucci, Escada, Tourneau, and Burberry. Along with Citrus restaurant, Hotel Valencia hosts the Vbar and Cielo.

After your day of shopping or after your business concludes in Silicon Valley, relax with a Cosmopolitan at the Vbar, one of the hottest, hippest bars in town. Enjoy your drink out in the sun and open air on the early California-style courtyard before heading across the flagstone to Citrus. There you'll find an elegant and intimate setting of warm colors, soft lighting, arched ceilings and palm fronds.

The restaurant offers a classic menu of steaks, chops and surf specials. You might begin dining on Warm Apple and Onion Tart or Tequila Shrimp with Orange Chimicuri and then enjoy Chef Paul Rohadfox's Rock Salt Crusted Prime Rib or Half Moon Bay Halibut.

Once finished, it's up to Cielo, the hotel rooftop, for wine and cheese or after dinner cocktails. The teak and canvas lounge seating is perfect for sitting by the firepit and watching a spectacular sunset or San Jose's sparkling nightlights. It's no wonder that Hotel Valencia (and Citrus) is considered one of the most romantic destinations in San Jose.

Seared Diver Scallops, Celeriac Purée, Black Trumpets with Sauce Vermeer

8 DIVER SCALLOPS   SERVES 4

❧ CELERIAC PURÉE

CELERIAC ROOTS PEELED, LARGE DICE

1 QT MILK

2 CUPS HEAVY CREAM

2 TBSP MASCARPONE CHEESE

1 TBSP SALT

1 TBSP BUTTER

❧ SAUCE VERMEER

2 OZ CALLEBAUT CHOCOLATE, SHAVED

1/4 CUP HEAVY CREAM

2 CUPS DEMI-GLACE

1/3 CUP VERMEER CHOCOLATE LIQUEUR

❧ TRUMPETS

6 OZ BLACK TRUMPET MUSHROOMS

3 TBSP DUCK FAT

(CAN BE SUBSTITUTED WITH OLIVE OIL)

2 TBSP PARSLEY, CHOPPED

2 SHALLOTS, SLICED THIN

❧ Place milk and salt in a pot and bring to a boil. Peel and cut celeriac root into large dice and place into pot. Reduce to medium heat and cook for 40 minutes or until soft. Remove from milk and place in a food processor. Purée until smooth (will not become smooth on the first purée). Remove and place into a pot. Gently heat. Slowly add heavy cream. Whisk to mashed potato consistency. (Do not add too much cream or celeriac will become loose). Return to food processor and purée a second time. Add mascarpone cheese into purée (this will give the purée its smooth texture). Place mixture into bowl. Add butter and season to taste. Keep warm.

❧ Heat demi-glace in a pan over medium heat making sure that demi does not boil. Slowly whisk in chocolate making sure chocolate melts before adding more. Add Vermeer and reduce heat. Cook for 4 minutes. Set aside.

Heat sauté pan just until smoking point. Chop herbs and set aside. Pat scallops dry making sure that there is no water on surface. Remove muscle from the scallops' sides. Season with salt and pepper. Place scallops, 3 at a time, in pan to ensure proper searing. (Too many scallops will reduce the searing temperature and cause the scallops to cook internally.) Sear for 4 to 5 minutes until light caramel color forms around bottom of scallop. Turn over and sear other side of scallop for 2 minutes. Set aside and keep warm.

28

In an additional sauté, pan heat duck fat (or olive oil). Add trumpets and sauté for 3 minutes. Add shallots and sauté for 3 more minutes. Remove from pan and toss with herbs. Return sauce to heat and add heavy cream. Whisk together. Finish by whisking in butter and adjust seasoning. Keep warm.

ASSEMBLY

Swirl sauce onto the plate using a back and forth motion. Spoon celeriac purée in the center of the plate. Place scallops on the side of the purée. Place trumpets gently on top of purée. Garnish with shaved chocolate. Serve immediately.

Roasted Beet and Asian Pear Salad

SERVES 4

Combine mustard, lemon juice and champagne vinegar in a bowl. Whisk all ingredients together. Slowly whisk in walnut oil until fully incorporated. Season with salt and pepper to taste.

Slice the cucumber lengthwise in thin strips, making sure you get a long, thin slice. (A slicer or mandolin is preferred for this preparation.) This will become a cucumber bowl.

Halve both of the pears. Remove the core. This step should be done right before the salad is served. (Do not do ahead of time or pear will discolor.) Slice pear very thinly and set aside right before serving.

Preheat oven to 350°. Trim the beets and wash with cool water. Toss gently with olive oil, salt and pepper. Place beets on sheet tray. Place in oven for 45 to 50 minutes. The beets are done when they can be pierced by a small knife with no resistance. Let beets begin to cool. When beets are almost cool, begin to rub off the skin with a towel. After beets are skinned, slice into 1/2" coin rounds. Set aside.

ASSEMBLY

Gently toss mache with a small amount of dressing and shallots. Make a circle with the lengthwise sliced cucumber (2 pieces may be required if the slices are not long enough). Place a small mound of the tossed salad into the middle of the cucumber bowl. Cascade beet rounds next to the salad. Sprinkle salad with small pieces of goat cheese and randomly sprinkle goat cheese around the plate. Gently place pears on top of the salad. Garnish with walnut halves and the remainder of the dressing.

6 RED BEETS
2 ASIAN PEARS
10 OZ BABY MACHE
6 OZ GOAT CHEESE
4 OZ WALNUTS, HALVED
3 OZ WALNUT VINAIGRETTE
1 CUCUMBER
4 TBSP OLIVE OIL

29

WALNUT VINAIGRETTE
4 TBSP DIJON MUSTARD
4 TBSP CHAMPAGNE VINEGAR
2 TBSP LEMON JUICE
1 1/2 CUPS WALNUT OIL
1 SHALLOT, MINCED
SALT AND PEPPER

Petite Angus Filet, Exotic Mushroom Mousse, Checkered Potato Salad, Roasted Shallot Confit with Port Wine Reduction

4 6 OZ ANGUS FILETS   SERVES 4

Preheat oven to 425°. Season filets lightly with salt and pepper. Set aside.

❧ CHECKERED POTATO SALAD
4 YUKON GOLD POTATOES
4 PURPLE PERUVIAN POTATOES
1/2 CUP BACON, DICED
1/2 CUP SCALLIONS, SLICED THIN
1 TSP THYME
1 TBSP PARSLEY
1/4 CUP MUSTARD AIOLI

❧ Peel potatoes and place in water to prevent discoloring. Cut potatoes into 1/2" cubes. Blanch potatoes in boiling water about 3 minutes. Remove and drain. Place potatoes into an ice bath approximately 2 minutes. Slice scallions on a bias. Set side for later use. Place bacon into a pan on medium heat, making sure that the bacon does not burn. Gently stir. Bacon should begin to crisp in about 10 minutes and oil should begin to double. At this point, the bacon can be removed to a plate lined with paper towels. Reserve bacon fat for later use. Chop parsley and thyme. Mix together and set aside.

❧ MUSTARD AIOLI
3 EGG YOLKS
3 TBSP WHOLE GRAIN MUSTARD
2 GARLIC CLOVES, CHOPPED
1 1/2 CUPS SALAD OIL OR VEGETABLE OIL
1 TBSP FRESH LEMON JUICE
4 OZ ICE WATER
SALT AND PEPPER

❧ Place egg yolks, garlic and lemon juice in a blender for 2 minutes. Add in mustard and blend for 1 minute. Slowly drizzle oil in a steady stream until a slightly thick consistency. Consistency can be adjusted by adding water if it becomes too thick. It should be pourable. Season to taste.

❧ ROASTED SHALLOT CONFIT
6 SHALLOTS, HALVED
3 TBSP OLIVE OIL
1 TBSP BROWN SUGAR
1/2 CUP RED WINE
1/3 CUP RED WINE VINEGAR

❧ Cut shallots in half. Sauté shallots in olive oil for approximately 10 minutes on low heat. Allow shallots to sweat and release natural juices. Add red wine, red wine vinegar and brown sugar. Cook for 5 minutes until liquid is slightly reduced. Place pan into 350° oven for 30 minutes, checking every 10 minutes. Remove shallots and stir. Keep warm.

❧ PORT WINE REDUCTION
3 CUPS RUBY PORT
3 SHALLOTS, SMALL DICED
1 QT DEMI-GLACE
2 TBSP BUTTER

❧ Slice shallots and sauté in butter on medium heat for 7 to 8 minutes without burning. Deglaze pan with port. Reduce by half, about 7 to 12 minutes. When reduced, add demi-glace. Reduce again by 1/3. After the sauce has reduced, adjust seasoning and keep warm.

❧ EXOTIC MUSHROOM MOUSSE
1 CUP OYSTER MUSHROOMS, CHOPPED
1 CUP CRIMINI MUSHROOMS, CHOPPED
1 CUP SHIITAKE MUSHROOMS, CHOPPED
2 TBSP BUTTER
3 TBSP OLIVE OIL
1 TBSP WHITE TRUFFLE OIL

❧ Sauté all mushrooms in butter together for 10 to 12 minutes until moisture has evaporated. Season with salt and pepper. Remove from heat and transfer to food processor. Blend till mixture is puréed. Slowly add cream cheese until fully incorporated. Pour into bowl. Fold in herbs and truffle oil. Set aside and keep cold.

(continued)

Heat medium size pan with olive oil to just before smoking point. Place filets in pan 2 at a time to ensure proper searing. Sear for 3 minutes. Turn over and sear for additional 2 minutes. Repeat this step for remaining filets. Spoon mousse over filets. Place in oven for 5 to 8 minutes for medium rare. Remove filets from oven and keep warm. Sauté potatoes in 2 tbsp of reserved bacon fat for 3 minutes. Add in bacon and cook for 1 minute. Place in bowl and add 2 tbsp of Mustard Aioli. Add herbs. Mix together, making sure potatoes are coated lightly.

1 TSP THYME LEAVES
1 TSP ROSEMARY LEAVES
1 TBSP PARSLEY
1 1/2 CUPS HEAVY CREAM
2 TBSP CREAM CHEESE

❖ GARNISH

CHIVES
COARSE BLACK PEPPER

ASSEMBLY

Place potato salad in middle of plate. Reheat shallots fully. Return sauce to heat. Add butter. Lean filet on top of the salad. Place shallot next to filet. Spoon sauce around the plate. Garnish with chives and sprinkle black pepper around the plate. Serve immediately.

Citrus Chocolate Cake

This flourless cake, meltingly soft on the inside, is served hot from the oven with freshly whipped cream, chocolate sauce and a garnish of candied orange peel.

SERVES 8

❖ CAKE

1/2 CUP (1 STICK) UNSALTED BUTTER, CUT INTO PIECES
PINCH OF SALT
15 OZ BITTERSWEET CHOCOLATE (VALRHONA RECOMMENDED), CHOPPED
4 EGG WHITES
1/2 CUP GRANULATED SUGAR
2 ORANGES, JUICED

❖ Preheat oven to 400°.

Lightly butter and sugar eight 3" disposable aluminum tins, 2" deep. In a large heavy saucepan and over low heat, melt the butter with the salt. Add the chocolate and stir over low heat until it is melted and the mixture is smooth. Be careful not to burn the chocolate. Let cool to room temperature.

In a large bowl, beat the egg whites until foamy. Gradually beat in the sugar until stiff and glossy peaks form. Fold the egg whites into the cooled chocolate. Add in the orange juice. Do not overmix or the batter will lose volume. Fill a pastry bag with batter. Pipe into the baking tins, filling each just over 1/2 full. Bake for 5 to 8 minutes. (It's important that the cakes are baked just before serving so the texture is correct. However, they can be made ahead and frozen before baking. Remove from freezer at least 1 hour before baking.)

❖ GARNISH

1 1/2 CUPS WHIPPING CREAM
1 TBSP CONFECTIONERS SUGAR, SIFTED
2 CUPS CHOCOLATE SAUCE
CANDIED ORANGE PEEL (OPTIONAL)
1 CUP BLUE CURACAO

ASSEMBLY

In a deep bowl, whip the cream with the confectioners sugar until stiff peaks form. Fill a pastry bag fitted with a star tip with the cream. Pipe rosettes around the outer circle of the plates. Cut orange peel into thin strips and set aside. Turn the warm cakes out onto the center of the plates. Pour chocolate sauce over the top and around the sides. Place orange peel on top of the cakes. Drizzle blue curacao around the plate. Serve immediately.

Wine Pairing

Seared Diver Scallops, Celeriac Purée,
Black Trumpets with Sauce Vermeer
2002 Ovation Chardonnay

Roasted Beet and Asian Pear Salad
2003 Sauvignon Blanc

Petite Angus Filet, Exotic Mushroom Mousse,
Checkered Potato Salad and Roasted Shallot Confit
with Port Wine Reduction
2000 Insignia

Citrus Chocolate Cake
2004 Eisrebe

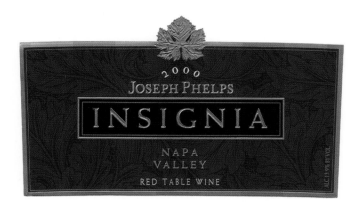

JOSEPH PHELPS
VINEYARD

JOSEPH PHELPS,
OWNER

200 TAPLIN ROAD

ST. HELENA, CA 94574

707.963.2745

WWW.JPVWINES.COM

IN 1973, JOE PHELPS ESTABLISHED AND BUILT THE WINERY WHICH bears his name and which over the years has become identified as one of the most respected benchmarks of California wine quality. "I'm very fortunate," he muses, "I've been able to combine the relaxed and less demanding lifestyle of farming with a fulfilling commitment to quality and a lifelong affection for fine wines."

The winery and home vineyards of Joseph Phelps are located in Spring Valley near St. Helena on a 600-acre ranch that is characterized by rolling hills, California native oaks and 95 acres of vines.

In addition to the home ranch, Joseph Phelps owns 225 acres of Napa Valley vineyards in the premiere growing regions of Stag's Leap, Rutherford, Oakville, Oak Knoll and the eastern foothills of Napa. In Sonoma County, an ambitious project was undertaken in 1999 to purchase land and develop vineyards along the western frontier of the Sonoma Coast, and today Joseph Phelps has 80 acres of Pinot Noir and 20 acres of Chardonnay planted in Freestone. Plans are underway for a small winery to be built in the midst of the Freestone vineyards.

Varietals produced annually at Joseph Phelps include Napa Valley Cabernet Sauvignon, Backus Vineyard Cabernet Sauvignon, Insignia (one of California's most successful first growth luxury blends), Chardonnay, Sauvignon Blanc, several Rhône-style wines and a luscious dessert wine made from Scheurebe.

Grilled Shrimp "Cobbs"mopolitan

Heirloom Tomatoes with a Laura Chenel Goat Cheese Sandwich

Pepper Seared Ahi on Lemon Jasmine Rice Salad with Tempura Green Beans, Wasabi and Ponzu

"Bada Bing" Cherry Crisp with Pistachio Gelato

Cosmopolitan

THE COSMOPOLITAN
STEVEN LEVINE,
CHEF

121 SPEAR STREET

SAN FRANCISCO, CA 94105

415.543.4001

WWW.THECOSMOPOLITANCAFE.COM

THE COSMOPOLITAN, ONE OF SAN FRANCISCO'S MOST ELEGANT AND HIP restaurants, is where Chef Steven Levine captivates his audience with his unique style of Contemporary American Cuisine. First class service from a well-orchestrated staff will satisfy your every need while dining in a sleek modern room with high ceilings, warm lighting and beautiful mahogany features. For a more casual atmosphere, The Cosmopolitan offers a bar lounge where you can enjoy Chef Levine's small bites accompanied by live piano and jazz every Wednesday through Friday night.

Using the finest local ingredients, Chef Levine is pleased to offer his signature Appetizer Trio—three different preparations that change daily and range from Hog Island Oysters to Foie Gras.

The Cosmopolitan has been rated in the Top 100 Restaurants in San Francisco for the last three years by the *San Francisco Chronicle*. Popular dishes include Crispy Duck Confit with Asian Pears and Point Reyes Blue Cheese, and Peppercorn Seared Ahi Tuna served with a lemon cilantro jasmine rice salad, tempura green beans and wasabi aoli. Baked-to-order desserts, such as the Banana Pecan Galette with bourbon gelato and Chef's famous Chocolate Trio, are some of the best in the city and not to be missed.

The Cosmopolitan's New World wine list offers selections from California, South Africa, New Zealand and South America. More than twenty different wines are available by the glass. It's not surprising that Cosmopolitan's wine list has received the Award of Excellence from *Wine Spectator*.

Grilled Shrimp "Cobbs" mopolitan

18 MEDIUM SHRIMP, PEELED
AND DEVEINED
1/4 CUP OLIVE OIL
2 TBSP EACH PARSLEY, THYME AND
TARRAGON, CHOPPED
SALT AND PEPPER TO TASTE
1 HEAD BIBB LETTUCE
1 HEAD RADICCHIO
2 HARDBOILED EGGS, CHOPPED
1/4 CUP CRISP BACON, DICED
1 AVOCADO, DICED
1/2 CUP GORGONZOLA, CRUMBLED
1/2 CUP SHALLOTS, SLICED THIN, COATED
WITH FLOUR, FRIED CRISP
9 CHERRY TOMATOES, SLICED IN HALF

✤ DRESSING
1/4 CUP SOUR CREAM
1/4 CUP BUTTERMILK
1/4 CUP MAYONNAISE
1/4 CUP RED WINE VINEGAR
1/4 CUP EXTRA VIRGIN OLIVE OIL
2 CLOVES GARLIC, CHOPPED
3 TBSP SHALLOTS, DICED
1/4 CUP GORGONZOLA, CRUMBLED
2 TBSP PARSLEY, CHOPPED
2 TBSP CHIVES, CHOPPED
1 TSP SALT
1/8 TSP FRESH GROUND BLACK PEPPER

SERVES 4

✤ For the dressing, combine all ingredients in a blender. Purée until smooth. Refrigerate for at least 1 hour.

Toss the shrimp with olive oil, herbs, and salt and pepper. Refrigerate for 1 hour.

When ready to serve, toss the bibb lettuce and radicchio leaves with the dressing. Place the leaves in a flower pattern in the middle of the plate. Top the leaves with hardboiled eggs, crisp bacon, diced avocado, gorgonzola and fried shallots. In a grill pan or on a barbeque, grill the shrimp for approximately 2 minutes on each side. Arrange the shrimp around the salad. Place cherry tomatoes around the plate.

36

Heirloom Tomatoes

with a

Laura Chenel

Goat Cheese Sandwich

SERVES 4-6

4-6 HEIRLOOM TOMATOES
GREY SEA SALT OR FLEUR DE SEL
FRESH GROUND BLACK PEPPER
1 BUNCH PICKED GREEN BASIL LEAVES
1 BUNCH PICKED OPAL BASIL LEAVES
1 BUNCH GREEN BASIL
1 CUP EXTRA VIRGIN OLIVE OIL
1 CUP BALSAMIC VINEGAR
1 CUP GRATED PARMESAN CHEESE
1/2 CUP FRESH LAURA CHENEL
GOAT CHEESE
4 TBSP HEAVY CREAM
4 TBSP EXTRA VIRGIN OLIVE OIL
MICRO GREENS FOR GARNISH

Preheat oven to 325°.

In a non-reactive pan and over medium heat, reduce the balsamic vinegar to about 2 tbsp. Refrigerate until cool.

Bring a small pot of lightly salted water to a boil. Blanch 1 bunch of green basil leaves. Cook for 10 seconds. Drain leaves. Cool in ice water until cold. Drain water.

In a blender, add blanched basil leaves and 1 cup extra virgin olive oil. Purée until smooth. Refrigerate for 1 hour.

In a mixer with a paddle attachment, add fresh goat cheese, heavy cream and 4 tbsp olive oil. Whip on medium speed until smooth. Set aside.

On a non-stick cookie sheet tray, sprinkle grated parmesan cheese in a 3" ring mold to form 12 thin circles. Bake in oven for 12 minutes. Cool at room temperature. Using a spatula, transfer cheese chips to paper towels. Set aside.

ASSEMBLY

When ready to serve, slice tomatoes. Toss in a bowl with the picked green and opal basil leaves. Season to taste with sea salt and pepper. Place in the middle of each plate, stacking one on top of the other. Spoon a little goat cheese between parmesan chips to form sandwiches. Place one sandwich on top of each plate of stacked tomatoes. Drizzle basil oil and balsamic syrup around the plates. Garnish with micro greens.

Pepper Seared Ahi on Lemon Jasmine Rice Salad
with Tempura Green Beans, Wasabi and Ponzu

6 6 OZ PORTIONS OF SASHIMI
GRADE AHI TUNA

1/4 CUP COARSE GROUND
BLACK PEPPERCORNS

1/4 CUP MIXED FRESH PARSLEY,
THYME AND TARRAGON, CHOPPED

1 TBSP KOSHER SALT

❖ TEMPURA BATTER
1 EGG YOLK

1 CUP ALL PURPOSE FLOUR

1 CUP COLD CLUB SODA

❖ WASABI MAYO
1/4 CUP WASABI POWDER

1/4 CUP WATER

2 TBSP RICE WINE VINEGAR

1/2 CUP MAYONNAISE

❖ PONZU
1/4 CUP LEMON JUICE

1/4 CUP LIME JUICE

1/4 CUP ORANGE JUICE

1 CUP LIGHT SOY SAUCE

1 CUP WATER

1 SHALLOT, DICED

1 JALAPEÑO, DICED

1" PIECE OF GINGER, DICED

❖ RICE SALAD
2 CUPS JASMINE RICE

3 CUPS WATER

1/4 CUP SCALLION, CHOPPED

1/4 CUP CILANTRO, CHOPPED

2 LEMONS, ZEST AND JUICE

1/4 CUP EXTRA VIRGIN OLIVE OIL

4 TBSP THAI FISH SAUCE

SALT AND PEPPER TO TASTE

❖ TEMPURA GREEN BEANS
54 BLUELAKE GREEN BEANS

1 QT CANOLA OIL FOR FRYING

TEMPURA BATTER

SERVES 6

❖ In a small bowl, add the egg yolk, 1/2 cup club soda and 1/2 cup flour. Mix slightly. Add remaining club soda and flour. Mix slightly, leaving mixture lumpy. Keep refrigerated until ready to use.

❖ In a small bowl, mix the wasabi powder, water and rice vinegar. Stir until smooth. Let sit for 15 minutes. Mix in the mayonnaise. Set aside.

❖ In a bowl, combine the lemon, lime and orange juices. Add soy sauce, water, shallot, jalapeño and ginger. Set aside.

❖ Bring 3 cups of water to a boil. Add 2 cups jasmine rice. Bring back to a boil. Cover and cook in a 350° oven for 15 minutes. Remove from oven. Let sit, covered, for 15 more minutes. Spread rice on a tray. Cover with a wet towel and cool to room temperature.

In a large bowl, combine cooled rice, grated lemon zest and juice, olive oil, fish sauce, scallions, cilantro, and salt and pepper. Set aside.

❖ Bring canola oil to 350° in a heavy bottom pot or tabletop fryer. Dip green beans in tempura batter. Fry in oil for 2 to 3 minutes or until slightly golden. Drain on paper towels. Keep warm.

Season tuna with salt, herbs and peppercorns. In a large skillet over high heat, put a few tablespoons of canola oil. Sear tuna on all sides. Slice tuna crosswise.

ASSEMBLY
In a large bowl, place rice salad in a 5" to 6" ring mold. Pat rice down. Set tuna on top of rice. Stack tempura beans on top of tuna. Drizzle wasabi mayo on top of beans. Pour Ponzu sauce around rice. Garnish with chopped chives.

"Bada Bing" Cherry Crisp with Pistachio Gelato

SERVES 4

Preheat oven to 350°.

In a large bowl, combine pitted cherries, port wine, red wine, sugar, lemon juice and zest, and cornstarch. Let sit for at least 1 hour to macerate.

In a mixing bowl with a paddle attachment, add oats, almonds, turbinado sugar, brown sugar, flour, salt and cinnamon. Mix on slow speed until combined. Add cold diced butter. Mix on slow speed until the mixture resembles pea size crumbs. Do not overmix.

In individual oven-safe bowls or soufflé dishes, add 4 oz of the cherry mixture. Sprinkle each with 1/4 cup almond streusel. Bake in oven for about 30 minutes. Top each crisp with a scoop of pistachio gelato. Garnish with powdered sugar and mint.

1 CUP PITTED BING CHERRIES
1/4 CUP RUBY PORT WINE
1/4 CUP RED WINE
1/4 CUP SUGAR
1 LEMON, ZEST AND JUICE
1 TBSP CORNSTARCH
1 CUP OLD FASHIONED OATS
1 CUP TURBINADO SUGAR
1/2 CUP LIGHT BROWN SUGAR
1/2 CUP ALL PURPOSE FLOUR
1/2 CUP CHOPPED ALMONDS
1 TSP GROUND CINNAMON
1/2 TSP SALT
4 OZ COLD BUTTER, DICED
6 SCOOPS PISTACHIO GELATO
POWDERED SUGAR AND MINT SPRIGS
FOR GARNISH

Wine Pairing

GRILLED SHRIMP "COBBS"MOPOLITAN
2004 NAPA VALLEY CHARDONNAY

HEIRLOOM TOMATOES
WITH A LAURA CHENEL GOAT CHEESE SANDWICH
2004 DURELL VINEYARD SONOMA VALLEY CHARDONNAY

PEPPER SEARED AHI ON LEMON JASMINE RICE SALAD
WITH TEMPURA GREEN BEANS, WASABI AND PONZU
2003 HYDE VINEYARD CARNEROS PINOT NOIR

"BADA BING" CHERRY CRISP
WITH PISTACHIO GELATO
2004 SONOMA COAST PINOT NOIR

40

PATZ & HALL
WINE COMPANY

JAMES HALL,
WINEMAKER AND OWNER
ANNE MOSES, DONALD PATZ,
AND HEATHER PATZ,
OWNERS

P.O. BOX 5479

NAPA, CA 94581

707.265.7700

WWW.PATZHALL.COM

THE PATZ & HALL WINE CO. IS THE CREATION OF FOUR INDIVIDUALS with an important diversity of experience and skills. While James Hall and Anne Moses focus on the crafting of consistently excellent Chardonnay and Pinot Noir, Donald Patz, Heather Patz and Anne look after sales and marketing. Together, they have created one of California's most lauded artisan wine brands.

Since founding Patz & Hall in early 1988, their goal has been to produce the finest quality Chardonnay and Pinot Noir in California. At that time, the paradigm of limited production, vineyard-focused wines that express the individuality of sites, clones, farming and winemaking methods was a leap forward for the California's emerging artisan wine business. From the beginning, Patz & Hall has sought out distinctive vineyards and then worked closely with the vineyard owners to grow the very best grapes to make their wines. This search has led them to exceptional vineyard sites in the Napa Valley, Russian River Valley, Mendocino County, Sonoma Coast and the Santa Lucia Highlands in Monterey County. Today, the Patz & Hall family of winegrowers continues to play an integral part in the success of this dynamic company.

The wines of Patz & Hall have set a standard for successfully balancing power and finesse. Vintage after vintage, Patz & Hall produces wines of distinct personality with dramatic flavors, seductive textures and a finely tuned harmony of tastes and aromas.

Seared Foie Gras, Spicy Poached Yellow Peach, White Peach Juice,
Tahitian Vanilla Butter

Sashimi of Kampachi, Geoduck, Watermelon Radish, Fresh Wasabi

Lamb Chops, Globe Squash Blossoms, Elephant Garlic Chips

Marshmallows

The Dining Room

THE DINING ROOM
AT THE RITZ-CARLTON
SAN FRANCISCO
RON SIEGEL,
CHEF DE CUISINE
ALEXANDER ESPIRITU,
PASTRY CHEF

600 STOCKTON STREET

SAN SRANCISCO, CA 94108

415.773.6168

WWW.RITZCARLTON.COM

THOSE ACCUSTOMED TO THE BEST ARE FAMILIAR WITH THE RITZ-CARLTON Hotels and the culinary excellence they offer in their restaurants. The Dining Room in The Ritz Carlton San Francisco is no exception. Few restaurants rival the elegance of The Dining Room in décor and in the masterful menu it serves. The Dining Room is one of only fourteen restaurants in North America to earn the coveted Five-Star Award from Exxon Mobil for 2005.

The intimate, candlelit atmosphere of The Dining Room perfectly complements Chef Ron Siegel's evolving menu, which focuses on modern French cuisine with a Japanese influence. Chef Siegel began his career at The French Laundry and he quickly became one of the Bay Area's rising culinary stars. In 1998, he defeated the reigning Iron Chef champion Hiroyuki Sakai on national television.

Your experience at The Dining Room begins when Sommelier Stephane Lacroix welcomes you with a glass of Champagne or sparkling wine from the custom-made Champagne cart. Then enjoy Chilled Dungeness Crab with mango and red onion compote before you savor the tenderness of the Dry Aged Beef Rib-Eye with bone marrow, asparagus, king trumpet mushrooms, truffle risotto and Bordelaise or the Black Bass with sautéed squid, caramelized baby fennel, sunchoke purée and sweet carrot glaze. Dinner guests may then select from over a dozen varieties of international and domestic cheeses made by local artisans followed by dessert temptations by Pastry Chef Alexander Espiritu.

Complete your perfect evening in surroundings fit for royalty as you sink onto the Egyptian cotton sheets, down comforter and feather bed in your suite at The Ritz-Carlton Hotel.

Seared Foie Gras, Spicy Poached Yellow Peach, White Peach Juice, Tahitian Vanilla Butter

❖ PICKLING

1/2 CUP CHAMPAGNE VINEGAR
1/2 CUP WATER
1 CUP SUGAR
1 CINNAMON STICK
10 CLOVES
14 BLACK PEPPERCORNS
8 ALLSPICE
1 STAR ANISE

4 3 OZ PORTIONS FOIE GRAS
2 WHOLE YELLOW PEACHES
(SLIGHTLY FIRM)
4 SLICES BRIOCHE
10 RIPE WHITE PEACHES
1/2 TAHITIAN VANILLA BEAN
4 OZ UNSALTED BUTTER, SOFTENED
SALT AND PEPPER
1 TBSP CHIVES, MINCED
FLEUR DU SEL

SERVES 4

❖ Toast all spices—cinnamon stick, cloves, black peppercorns, allspice, star anise—until aromatic, about 2 minutes. Wrap spices in cheesecloth and tie to secure. Set aside.

Bring sugar, water and vinegar to a boil, stirring constantly to avoid scorching. Once boiled, add toasted spices. Let simmer.

Blanche yellow peaches in boiling water for 5 seconds. Shock in ice bath. Peel skin. Set aside.

Slice peaches in half, discarding pit. Gently place peaches in pickling liquid for approximately 10 minutes or until peaches becomes slightly soft. Remove from heat and set aside.

Cut brioche into desired shapes. Toast in a sauté pan with 1 tbsp of butter. Purée remaining butter with seeds of the vanilla bean. Pass through tami.

Remove pit from 10 ripe peaches. Juice through a juicer. Strain through a chinois. Place in a saucepot over medium heat. Reduce by half. Strain back through a chinois.

Season both sides of foie gras with salt and pepper. Sear in smoking hot pan (do not add oil) until golden brown on both sides. Remove and place on half sheet tray over paper towels. Place in 425° oven for approximately 3 minutes or until hot.

ASSEMBLY

Reheat peach juice and slowly whisk in vanilla butter. Once hot, distribute evenly into 4 bowls. Place brioche on top. Add hot peach to top of brioche. Remove foie gras from oven and place on top of peach. Garnish with fleur de sel and minced chives. Serve immediately.

44

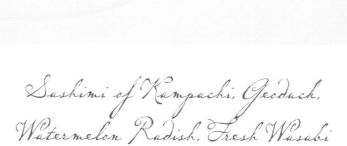

Sashimi of Kampachi, Geoduck, Watermelon Radish, Fresh Wasabi

SERVES 4

Slice Kampachi paper thin. Divide into 4 portions and place on serving plates. Season lightly with salt and pepper. Julienne watermelon radish. Chiffonode the geoduck. Add to watermelon radish. Season to taste with lemon oil, wasabi and salt and pepper. Sprinkle with minced Kaisou and serve immediately.

8 OZ KAMPACHI
1 TBSP GEODUCK
1 WATERMELON RADISH
1 TBSP KAISOU, FINELY MINCED
LEMON OLIVE OIL TO TASTE
WASABI TO TASTE
SALT AND PEPPER

Lamb Chops, Globe Squash Blossoms, Elephant Garlic Chips

✤ LAMB SERVES 4

2 FRENCH LAMB RACKS

✤ ELEPHANT GARLIC CHIPS

1 HEAD ELEPHANT GARLIC

2 CUPS VEGETABLE OIL

✤ SQUASH BLOSSOMS

4 CLOVES REGULAR GARLIC

2 LARGE SHALLOTS

3 TBSP OLIVE OIL

6 GLOBE SQUASH

12 SQUASH BLOSSOMS

1 BUNCH BASIL

1 OZ UNSALTED BUTTER

2 OZ PARMESAN CHEESE

SALT AND PEPPER

✤ Split lamb racks into chops. Season with salt and pepper on both sides. Sear in hot pan with olive oil. Cook until desired temperature is reached. Set aside.

✤ Slice elephant garlic into rounds for chips on Japanese mandolin and place in pot of cold water. Bring to boil and blanch. Remove and place on paper towels.

Heat 2 cups of vegetable oil to 325° in a large pot. Add garlic chips and cook until light golden brown. Remove and season with salt.

✤ Mince the garlic and shallots together. Sweat in olive oil in sauté pan. Split globe squash in half, then in half-moons. Add to the garlic and shallots. Tie the bunch of basil with string. Add to squash. Cook until squash breaks down. Add butter and Parmesan cheese. Season to taste and remove from heat. Stuff squash blossoms with prepared stuffing. Set aside.

ASSEMBLY

Heat stuffed squash blossoms on sheet pan in 425° oven. Once hot, serve each blossom with lamb chops. Place garlic chips on top of each chop and serve immediately.

46

Marshmallows

4 DOZEN

3 TBSP + 2 TSP GELATIN
2 1/4 CUPS WATER
3 TSP ORANGE WATER
(AVAILABLE AT MOST
MIDDLE EASTERN STORES OR
MAY SUBSTITUTE WITH
GRAND MARNIER)
3 1/4 CUPS SUGAR
1 CUP GLUCOSE
(AVAILABLE AT ALL PHARMACIES)
1 1/4 CUPS CORN SYRUP
1/4 CUP CORNSTARCH
1/4 CUP POWDERED SUGAR

In mixing bowl, soak gelatin with orange blossom water or Grand Marnier and 1 cup water. Set aside.

Place sugar, glucose, corn syrup and remaining 1 1/4 cups water in a large copper pot. Cover and place on high heat. Once sugar mixture begins to boil, remove the lid and continue to cook until mixture reaches 252°. Once desired temperature is reached, remove from flame and cool to 210°.

Melt the gelatin mixture in a bowl in the microwave. Using the whisk attachment to your stand mixer, slowly add the sugar mixture. Mix on high speed until medium peaks form. Using a rubber spatula sprayed with non-stick cooking spray, transfer the marshmallow onto a 12"x 17" sheet pan covered with oiled parchment paper. Place a second sheet of oiled parchment on top. Using a rolling pin, roll out mixture to be an even height of 1". Let sit overnight.

Remove the top sheet of parchment from the marshmallow. Sprinkle with equal parts powdered sugar and cornstarch. Using a warm knife, cut into 1" squares.

May be kept in airtight container for 1 week.

Wine Pairing

Seared Foie Gras, Spicy Poached Yellow Peach,
White Peach Juice, Tahitian Vanilla Butter
Vin de Paille "Quintessence" 2003,
Paso Robles

Sashimi of Kampachi, Geoduck,
Watermelon Radish, Fresh Wasabi
Esprit de Beaucastel Blanc 2003,
Paso Robles

Lamb Chops, Globe Squash Blossoms,
Elephant Garlic Chips
Esprit de Beaucastel 2002,
Paso Robles

Marshmallows
Vin de Paille 2003,
Paso Robles

48

TABLAS CREEK VINEYARD

2003 ESPRIT de BEAUCASTEL BLANC

GROWN & BOTTLED ON THE ESTATE

PASO ROBLES

Roussanne 68%
Grenache Blanc 27%, Viognier 5%

750ML · ALCOHOL 14.5% BY VOLUME

TABLAS CREEK VINEYARD

HAAS VINEYARD COMPANY AND PERRIN VINEYARD COMPANY, OWNERS

9339 ADELAIDA ROAD

PASO ROBLES, CA 93446

805.237.1231

WWW.TABLASCREEK.COM

THE PERRIN FAMILY OF CHÂTEAU DE BEAUCASTEL AND ROBERT HAAS, longtime importer and owner of Vineyard Brands, founded Tablas Creek Vineyard in the hilly Las Tablas district of west Paso Robles. They chose this location because of its similarities to Châteauneuf du Pape—limestone soils, a favorable climate and the rugged terrain.

The partners imported the traditional varietals grown on the Perrins' celebrated estate including Mourvèdre, Grenache Noir, Syrah and Counoise for reds; and Roussanne, Viognier, Marsanne and Grenache Blanc for whites. These imported vines passed a rigorous three-year USDA testing program and are propagated and grafted in an on-site nursery. All Tablas Creek wines are estate grown and organically farmed.

Tablas Creek follows the centuries-old Châteauneuf du Pape tradition of blending chosen varietals, which produces wines that are more complex, better balanced and richer than single varietal wines. Each varietal is hand-harvested when completely ripe and fermented separately. Winemaking, including native yeast fermentation and neutral French oak barrels, preserves the wines' ties to their soil, climate and varietal character.

The Vineyard's signature wines are the Esprit de Beaucastel, based on Mourvèdre, and Esprit de Beaucastel Blanc, based on Roussanne. These wines are designed to be rich, balanced and ageable, and should reward maturation time in bottle. The Vineyard also produces the Côtes de Tablas, based on Grenache, and the Côtes de Tablas Blanc, based on Viognier, as well as several other varietal wines.

Warm Poached Ranch Egg with American Black Caviar

Dungeness Crab Stuffed Rouget with Local Asparagus and Red Wine Gastrique

Milk Poached Local Halibut with Ruby Beet Carpaccio, Spring Onions, Watercress and Tangerine

Gooey Chocolate Caramel Cake with Vanilla Cream

Farallon

FARALLON

MARK FRANZ,
OWNER AND
EXECUTIVE CHEF
PAT KULETO,
OWNER
PARKE ULRICH,
CHEF DE CUSINE
EMILY LUCHETTI,
EXECUTIVE PASTRY CHEF
JENNIFER CREAGER,
PASTRY CHEF

450 POST STREET

SAN FRANCISCO, CA 94102

415.956.6969

WWW.FARALLONRESTAURANT.COM

AN UNDERSEA WORLD THAT CAN ONLY BE DESCRIBED AS JULES VERNE'S imagination brought-to-life, Farallon is in a class of its own. Glass sculptured sea creatures suspend above you, velvet booths encompass you and delectable gifts from the sea (and land) await you. Enter Farallon. The front room seating plays host to the 'jelly' bar whose backdrop of sculpted fish scales and kelp-twined columns sets the mood. A sweeping staircase arises to the mezzanine where you can sit and look down upon Farallon's sea below.

The main dining room is a re-creation of what you envision as the view from Nemo's Nautilus; even the booths mimic the undersea world. In keeping with its water theme, beneath the 1926 arched ceilings and mosaic tiled floor still sits the original swimming pool of the Elks Lodge.

Farallon is the acclaimed collaboration between Chef Mark Franz and imaginative restaurateur and designer Pat Kuleto. They bring their talents together to create a truly unique environment and culinary experience. Chef Franz gives new meaning to the term 'coastal cuisine' with his menu of wild and farmed fish from all over the world, including a few varieties from the fish-rich waters around the Farallon Islands, thirty miles west of the Golden Gate. His Cornmeal Battered Gulf Shrimp and Serrano Ham Roasted Rainbow Trout provide flavors you won't have experienced before and will look forward to enjoying again.

Don't leave this oceanic wonderland without finishing with one of Pastry Chef Emily Luchetti's renowned desserts including Small Endings, an extraordinary sampling of her assorted handmade confections and the perfect ending to your dining experience beneath the sea.

Warm Poached Ranch Egg
with American Black Caviar

4 ORGANIC EGGS

1 QT WATER

1 TBSP DISTILLED VINEGAR

2 OZ EXTRA VIRGIN OLIVE OIL

8 SLICES BRIOCHE

2 OZ BLACK CAVIAR

2 TBSP CHIVES, MINCED

SERVES 4

In a medium saucepan, bring water and vinegar to a simmer, approximately 190°. Crack the eggs. Soft poach the eggs for 4 minutes or until desired doneness. Remove with a slotted spoon and pat the bottom of the spoon on a clean kitchen towel to remove any excess water. Place eggs in the center of a small plate.

While the egg is poaching, toast the brioche and cut into toast points. Drizzle olive oil over and around the eggs. Top with caviar. Serve brioche on the side and sprinkle chives over caviar to garnish. Serve while the eggs are still warm.

52

Dungeness Crab Stuffed Rouget with Local Asparagus and Red Wine Gastrique

SERVES 4

4 WHOLE ROUGET (RED MULLET)
5 OZ DUNGENESS CRABMEAT
2 OZ GRAPESEED OIL
(OR OTHER OIL FOR SAUTÉ)
8 JUMBO ASPARAGUS, PEELED
EXTRA VIRGIN OLIVE OIL, AS NEEDED
1 CUP PORT WINE
1 CUP GOOD QUALITY RED WINE
2 TBSP ORANGE JUICE
1/2 CUP SUGAR
BUTCHER TWINE
SALT AND PEPPER TO TASTE
FRESH PICKED HERBS
(I.E., DILL, BASIL, THYME)

Preheat oven to 400°.

In a small saucepan, combine wines, orange juice and sugar. Place over medium heat and reduce to a syrup. Cool and reserve.

Remove the backbone of the rouget by fileting through the belly, keeping the head and tail intact. Using kitchen shears, clip the backbone out and pull the pin bones out with tweezers. Season the inside cavity of the fish and stuff with some of the crabmeat.

Gently tie the body of the rouget twice around with butcher's twine. Preheat a sauté pan over medium high heat. Add grapeseed oil or other sautéing oil. Season rouget with salt and pepper. Gently place in the pan. Place pan in the oven and cook for 4 minutes.

While fish is cooking, place asparagus in boiling salted water and boil until tender, about 3 minutes. Remove. Season with salt and pepper and toss in extra virgin olive oil.

ASSEMBLY

Place asparagus spears on plate. Place rouget on the plate so it looks as if it is swimming between the asparagus. Drizzle reserved red wine reduction around the fish. Top each fish with warmed crabmeat and picked herbs.

Milk Poached Local Halibut with Ruby Beet Carpaccio, Spring Onions, Watercress and Tangerine

❖ BEET CARPACCIO

SERVES 4

5 BABY BEETS OF DIFFERENT COLORS
(RUBY, GOLD, CHIOGGA-PINK)
1 TBSP OLIVE OIL
SALT AND PEPPER
1 TSP FRESH THYME LEAVES
1/2 CUP WATER

❖ Preheat oven to 400°.

Place beets in a small baking dish. Rub with oil, and salt and pepper. Add thyme and water and cover with a lid or aluminum foil. Roast until tender, about 45 minutes. Uncover and let cool before removing skins. Slice ruby red beets across into very thin coins and reserve. Quarter remaining beets and reserve.

❖ SPRING ONIONS

6 BULBS YOUNG SPRING ONIONS
1 TSP OLIVE OIL
1 TSP FRESH THYME, CHOPPED
2 TBSP CORNSTARCH OR RICE FLOUR
3 OZ CANOLA OR GRAPESEED OIL
SALT AND PEPPER

❖ On the onions, trim any roots from the bottom and trim off the green tops. Using 3 or 4 of the onions, cut 1/4" thick rings. Marinate the onion rings in olive oil and chopped thyme. Season with salt and pepper. Roast on a sheet pan in the oven for 4 minutes.

Thinly shave the remaining whole onions. Toss the onion shavings gently in cornstarch to coat and strain out excess cornstarch. Warm canola oil in a small saucepan. Carefully drop onions into oil to fry. As onions just start to turn golden, remove from oil and place on a towel to absorb excess oil. Season with salt and pepper and reserve in a warm place so they remain crispy.

❖ TANGERINE VINAIGRETTE

2 SATSUMA TANGERINES
2 OZ EXTRA VIRGIN
OLIVE OIL
SALT AND PEPPER

❖ Grate the skin of the tangerine to remove the zest and reserve. With a knife, remove the remaining skin. Cut out the tangerine sections from the membrane and mix with the zest. Pulverize the tangerine segments with a whisk. Add olive oil and season with salt and pepper.

2 CUPS WATERCRESS
2 TBSP CHIVES, CHOPPED

❖ HALIBUT

4 6 OZ PORTIONS
HALIBUT FILET,
SKIN ON
BUTTER FOR SAUTÉ
4 OZ WHOLE MILK
1 OZ GOOD QUALITY
WHITE WINE
SALT AND PEPPER

❖ Season the halibut filets with salt and pepper. Place skin-side-up in a lightly buttered sauté pan. Add milk and gently heat to a simmer. Place a lid on top. Place in the preheated oven for 5 minutes. Remove the lid, being careful of the steam. Remove the skin from the fish by gently pulling across the filet, not straight up. Flip the filet over so bottom side is now up. Reserve warm.

ASSEMBLY

Place ruby red beet coins flat on a plate in a circular form. Mix the quartered beets with the roasted spring onions and watercress. Dress lightly with Tangerine Viniagrette and season to taste. Place equal amounts of warm salad among the 4 plates. Drizzle vinaigrette around

54

the beets. Place halibut on top of the salad and garnish with fried spring onion rings.

Gooey Chocolate Caramel Cake with Vanilla Cream

SERVES 6

❖ Preheat oven to 350°.

Butter and sugar the insides of six 4 oz ramekins or muffin cups. Sift cocoa powder, flour, baking powder and salt. Cream butter and sugar until light. Add eggs, one at a time.

Combine vanilla extract, buttermilk and water. Alternate adding dry and wet ingredients in 3 additions. Mix until combined. Scrape bottom of the bowl to ensure that batter is completely mixed.

Divide the batter between the prepared ramekins. Bake in the oven for about 35 minutes or until a skewer inserted in the center comes out clean. The cakes should be served warm, and they can be reheated. Store at room temperature.

❖ Stir together the water, sugar and corn syrup in a pot. Cook over medium heat until the sugar is dissolved. Increase to high heat and cook until light golden. Do not stir after it comes to a boil. Remove from heat.

Carefully stir in the cream, a little at a time. (Be careful, as the caramel will sputter as the cream is added.) After all the cream has been added, stir in the remaining ingredients. Return to heat. Cook at medium heat, stirring occasionally, until caramel is a deep golden brown, about 4 minutes. This sauce should be served warm. It can be reheated in a microwave or double boiler.

❖ Whip cream, sugar and vanilla to medium-stiff peaks. Fold in caramel. Refrigerate until ready to serve

ASSEMBLY

Warm the caramel sauce. Place a chocolate cake on each plate. Pour some of the caramel sauce over and around the top. Spoon cream on the side. Garnish with the toasted almonds.

❖ CAKE
1/2 CUP COCOA POWDER
3/4 FLOUR
1/8 TSP BAKING POWDER
1/4 TSP SALT
4 OZ BUTTER, SOFT
1 CUP SUGAR
2 EGGS
1/2 TSP VANILLA EXTRACT
1/3 CUP BUTTERMILK
1 1/2 TBSP WATER

❖ CARAMEL SAUCE
1/2 CUP WATER
1 CUP SUGAR
1/2 CUP CORN SYRUP
1 OZ BUTTER
1 CUP CREAM
LARGE PINCH OF SALT
1/2 TSP VANILLA EXTRACT

❖ VANILLA CREAM
1 CUP HEAVY WHIPPING CREAM
1 TBSP SUGAR
1/2 TSP VANILLA EXTRACT

1/2 CUP SLICED ALMONDS
WITH SKINS ON, TOASTED

55

WARM POACHED RANCH EGG WITH AMERICAN BLACK CAVIAR
2003 OLD VINES CHENIN BLANC,
ERNESTO WICKENDEN VINEYARD

DUNGENESS CRAB STUFFED ROUGET
WITH LOCAL ASPARAGUS AND RED WINE GASTRIQUE
2002 CHARDONNAY,
TINAQUAIC VINEYARD OR
2003 PINOT NOIR,
SANTA MARIA VALLEY

MILK POACHED LOCAL HALIBUT
WITH RUBY BEET CARPACCIO, SPRING ONIONS,
WATERCRESS AND TANGERINE
2003 CHARDONNAY,
TINAQUAIC VINEYARD

GOOEY CHOCOLATE CARAMEL CAKE WITH VANILLA CREAM
2000 FORTIFIED MISSION

FOXEN

RICHARD DORÉ AND
BILL WATHEN,
OWNERS

7200 FOXEN CANYON ROAD

SANTA MARIA, CA 93454

805.937.4251

WWW.FOXENVINEYARD.COM

FOXEN'S WINERY AND TASTING ROOM WAS CALLED "RUSTIC AT BEST" by *Wine Spectator*. Rustic, yes—but that's the way FOXEN likes it.

Owners Bill Wathen and Dick Doré have been making wine together since 1985 when they founded FOXEN at the historic Rancho Tinaquaic in northern Santa Barbara County. Since that time, their focus has remained the same—the creation of very small production, vineyard designated wines using a "minimalist" approach to winemaking.

The winery is named in memory of William Benjamin Foxen, an English sea captain and Dick's great-great grandfather, who came to Santa Barbara in the early 1800s. In 1837, this Santa Barbara County pioneer purchased Rancho Tinaquaic, a Mexican land grant, and adopted the distinctive "anchor" as his ranch's cattle brand which later became a trademark of the winery. It's fitting that FOXEN makes its home on the now 2000-acre Rancho Tinaquaic, which remains in the Doré family hands.

Although best known for their outstanding Pinot Noirs from the Bien Nacido, Julia's and Sea Smoke Vineyards, FOXEN also takes advantage of Santa Barbara's diverse microclimates by creating a number of other highly-acclaimed wines including Chenin Blanc, Chardonnay, Syrah, Cabernet and a new Cabernet Franc/Merlot blend known as Foothills Reserve.

The "Foxen boys" invite you to visit their winery and tasting room, enjoy their limited production wines, play with the dogs and enjoy the beautiful rural setting. You will then understand why people say, "If you don't know FOXEN, you don't know Dick...or Bill."

Spiny Lobster with Meyer Lemon Risotto

Roasted Lamb Loin and Lacquered Rib

Winter Squash and Sage

Chocolate Velvet Cake with Caramel Swirl Ice Cream

FIFTH FLOOR
MELISSA PERELLO,
EXECUTIVE CHEF

12 FOURTH STREET,
5TH FLOOR
SAN FRANCISCO, CA 94103
415.348.1555
WWW.HOTELPALOMAR.COM

ATOP THE SOPHISTICATED HOTEL PALOMAR (CONSIDERED BY *Travel & Leisure* one of the greatest hotels and resorts in the world) in the heart of Union Square sits the celebrated Fifth Floor. The restaurant features Chef Melissa Perello's award-winning modern French cuisine. At just 28, Melissa is one of the Bay Area's most prominent chefs, having been named a *San Francisco Chronicle* Rising Star and one of *Food & Wine*'s 10 Best New Chefs in 2004.

The dining room is a perfect match for the menu. You dine in splendor on velvet banquettes or ebony chairs atop a zebra-print carpet surrounded by original modern art from San Francisco's Dolby Chadwick Gallery. The stylish surroundings are very urban and very comfortable—an ideal fit for Chef Perello's California inspired French cooking and fresh daily menu.

The Fifth Floor also has the distinction of featuring all-female professionals. Joining Chef Perello are Sommelier Emily Wines and Pastry Chef Marika Doob. Between them and the excellent service, the Fifth Floor can turn your dining experience into one of the finest San Francisco has to offer.

Spiny Lobster with Meyer Lemon Risotto

1/4 CUP WHITE WINE VINEGAR
2 CUPS WHITE WINE
2 1 1/4 LB SPINY LOBSTERS, LIVE
2 TBSP CANOLA OIL
4 LARGE TOMATOES, QUARTERED
1 1/2 CUPS CARNAROLI
OR ARBORIO RICE
3 TBSP EXTRA VIRGIN OLIVE OIL
1/2 YELLOW ONION, MINCED
3 CUPS CHICKEN BROTH
OR STOCK, BOILING
SALT AND WHITE PEPPER
3 TBSP BUTTER
1/4 CUP MASCARPONE CHEESE
ZEST AND JUICE OF 1 MEYER LEMON
1/2 BUNCH BABY DILL,
BROKEN INTO SPRIGS

SERVES 4

In a large pot, bring 1 quart water, the vinegar and the white wine to a rapid boil. Immerse lobsters and turn off heat. Let stand for 10 minutes. Remove lobsters and cool briefly in iced water. Drain when cool to touch. Reserve 1/4 cup of the cooking liquid ("court boullion") and discard the remainder. Separate the lobster heads from the tails by twisting the two in opposite directions. Drain any remaining liquid from the heads. Tear or cut each head into 6 pieces and reserve. Gently remove the tail meat from the shell and again reserve the shells. Split the two tails in half lengthwise. Rinse and set the tails aside.

Heat a medium saucepan and add the canola oil. When smoke begins to appear, add the reserved lobster shells and reduce the heat moderately. Stir frequently until shells achieve a deep red and golden hue. Add the tomatoes. Continue to cook slowly until the rendered liquid is fully reduced. Add 1 quart cold water and simmer for 1 1/2 hours or until reduced by half. Strain the remaining liquid, discarding the shells. Continue to reduce in a clean saucepan until 1/4 cup of the liquid ("lobster sauce") remains.

In a medium saucepan over low to medium heat, sweat the onion and olive oil until translucent. Add the rice and stir to coat. Season with 2 tsp salt. Add the chicken stock, 1/2 cup at a time, stirring constantly. Once the rice absorbs the stock, add an additional 1/2 cup stock until you have used all of it. Cover the pan with a tight lid or foil. Set aside until you are ready to serve.

Bring the remaining 1/4 cup of court bouillon to a simmer. Gently stir in the butter until completely melted and partly emulsified. Turn the heat off. Add the 4 lobster halves to the pan, white side down.

Return the risotto to the stove on low heat. Add the lemon zest. Adjust the seasoning with salt, white pepper and lemon juice. Add the mascarpone cheese and stir until incorporated. Briefly flip the lobster tails over onto the "red side." If necessary, turn the heat back on to warm the lobsters.

Spoon 1 tbsp of the lobster sauce onto each plate. Top with 1 large spoonful of the risotto. Place 1 lobster tail on each plate. Garnish with baby dill and a drizzle of lemon-infused or extra virgin olive oil.

Roasted Lamb Loin and Lacquered Rib

SERVES 4

1 RACK OF LAMB
(7 TO 9 BONES),
CHINE BONE OFF
NOT FRENCHED
1/4 CUP BREWED COFFEE
2 SPRIGS FRESH THYME
1 SMALL CLOVE GARLIC,
CRUSHED
2 SPRIGS FRESH SAGE
VEGETABLE OIL
1 TSP BUTTER
SALT AND PEPPER

Preheat oven to 350°. Remove the outermost cap of fat from the lamb (fat should peel off quite easily without any need for cutting). Remove the bones or "ribs" by sliding your knife down the inner side of the bones. Beginning at the most narrow section of the meat, follow all the way down the bottom of the loin. (It is beneficial to leave a small amount of meat on the ribs by not following the bones too closely.) Trim the remaining loin section of excess fat (silver skin). Season the ribs and the loin generously with salt and pepper.

Place the ribs of the lamb into a large resealable zip-lock bag. Add the coffee, thyme and garlic. Seal the bag, removing as much air as possible. Place the bag in a 170° to 200° water bath for approximately 4 hours or until the bones gently release from the meat. Place the unopened bag in an ice bath and cool for 20 minutes. Remove the lamb from the bag. Reserve all of the remaining liquid. Gently rinse the ribs with cold water. Pat dry with a paper towel. Cut the ribs into 3 equal sections and reserve. Place the liquid into a small saucepan with 2 sprigs of fresh sage. Reduce by half. Occasionally skim excess fat from the top. Reserve.

Sear the seasoned loin in a hot pan with vegetable oil until golden on all sides. Finish the loin in the oven to your desired temperature. Let the meat rest for several minutes before slicing. Meanwhile, sear the ribs in a hot pan with vegetable oil until golden brown. Drain excess liquid from the pan. Add 1 tsp butter to the reserved cooking liquid and lightly glaze the ribs.

ASSEMBLY

Slice the loin meat into 1/4" slices. Place a section of rib on each plate. Drizzle with the reserved cooking liquid. Rest 3 or 4 slices of the loin meat alongside. Serve with Winter Squash and Sage.

61

Winter Squash & Sage

6" SLICES ROUGE D'TAMPE PUMPKIN

1 ACORN OR DELICATA SQUASH,
QUARTERED

SALT AND COARSELY GROUND
BLACK PEPPER

WHITE PEPPER

BUTTER

10 SPRIGS FRESH SAGE,
PLUS ADDITIONAL CHOPPED

SERVES 4

Gently season pumpkin and squash with salt and white pepper. Place a small piece of butter and 2 sprigs of sage on top of each piece. Place each piece of squash into separate unsealed plastic bags. Microwave each bag separately on medium high heat for 2 minutes on each side. Cool. When cool, remove the flesh of each piece from the skin. Discard the skin, seeds and sage. Cut the remaining flesh into 1" cubes. Reserve.

Heat a small pan with a small amount of clarified butter. Add the diced squash. Sauté slowly until squash is golden and soft. Season with salt and black pepper. Add 1 tbsp butter. Allow the butter to achieve a golden brown color. Finish with a pinch of chopped sage.

62

Chocolate Velvet Cake with Caramel Swirl Ice Cream

❖ CARAMEL

10 PIECES PREPARED CARAMELS

3 TBSP CREAM

❖ CARAMEL SWIRL
ICE CREAM

3 CUPS HEAVY CREAM

1 CUP WHOLE MILK

1 VANILLA BEAN
(OR 2 TSP VANILLA EXTRACT)

10 EGG YOLKS

3/4 CUP PLUS 2 TBSP SUGAR

PINCH OF SALT

SERVES 6

❖ Unwrap caramels and place into a very small saucepan. Add the cream. Place over low heat, stirring frequently until melted and smooth. Remove from the heat. Store at room temperature until needed. Before use, if the caramel is too hard, gently heat it until just warm to the touch. Half of the caramel will be used for the Caramel Swirl Ice Cream and the other half will be drizzled over the cakes.

❖ Combine the cream, milk and vanilla bean in a medium-size saucepan. Place over moderate heat until just steaming. Whisk the egg yolks with the sugar until lightened in color. Slowly add half of the heated cream mixture to the yolks while whisking constantly. Pour this mixture back into the pot. Cook over low heat until the custard coats the back of a spoon. Chill immediately in an ice bath until cold (if using vanilla extract, add it here). Keep refrigerated until ready to spin. Spin according to the manufacturer's instructions. Place the spun ice cream into a container. Drizzle some of the caramel over it. Using a spoon, gently swirl the caramel into the ice cream once or twice. Drizzle more of the caramel and swirl again. (Do not overmix the caramel into the ice cream or the "swirl" will not be noticeable.) Store in the freezer for several hours or until ready to use.

❖ Combine all the ingredients in a heatproof bowl. Place over steaming water. Mix occasionally until melted and smooth. Store at room temperature until needed or refrigerate and reheat when ready to serve.

❖ Preheat oven to 275°.

Moderately coat a non-stick standard size muffin pan with vegetable spray. Cut rounds of parchment paper to fit the bottom of each mold (or you can use paper cup liners). Fill a medium size pot halfway up with water. Bring to a boil. Reduce heat so the water is steaming but not simmering. In a heatproof bowl (large enough to fit over the pot), combine the milk, cream, chocolate, cocoa powder, butter and sugar. Place the bowl over the steaming water. Mix often until melted and smooth. Remove the bowl from the heat. Sift the dry ingredients together. Add to the chocolate mixture. Mix until smooth. Whisk in the egg and vanilla extract. Fill 6 of the molds halfway up with the batter. Bake for 12 minutes. Rotate the pan, then bake another 8 minutes. Remove from the oven. Cool 5 to 10 minutes.

ASSEMBLY

Place a chocolate cake in the middle of each plate. Drizzle caramel and chocolate sauces over the cakes. Top with chopped toffee and a scoop of Caramel Swirl Ice Cream.

❖ CHOCOLATE SAUCE

1/2 CUP (3 OZ) SEMISWEET CHOCOLATE, CHOPPED

1 TBSP UNSALTED BUTTER

1/4 CUP HEAVY CREAM

❖ CHOCOLATE VELVET CAKE

1/4 CUP MILK

2 TBSP HEAVY CREAM

1/3 CUP (2 OZ) SEMISWEET CHOCOLATE, CHOPPED

2 TBSP UNSWEETENED COCOA POWDER

4 TBSP (2 OZ.) UNSALTED BUTTER

1/3 CUP SUGAR

1/3 CUP PLUS 1 TBSP ALL-PURPOSE FLOUR

1/4 TSP BAKING SODA

1/8 TSP BAKING POWDER

PINCH OF SALT

1 EGG

1/2 TSP VANILLA EXTRACT

TOFFEE, CHOPPED INTO SMALL PIECES

63

SPINY LOBSTER WITH MEYER LEMON RISOTTO
2002 SANFORD AND BENEDICT CHARDONNAY

WINTER SQUASH AND SAGE
2001 "HILDEGARD" ESTATE BOTTLED WHITE TABLE WINE

ROASTED LAMB LOIN AND LACQUERED RIB
2001 "ISABELLE MORGAN" PINOT NOIR

CHOCOLATE VELVET CAKE WITH CARAMEL SWIRL ICE CREAM
1994 "PRONTO" DESSERT ALEATICO

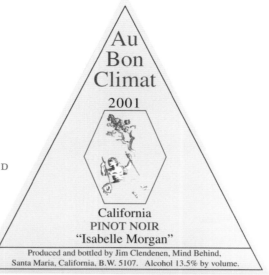

Jᴉᴍ Cʟᴇɴᴅᴇɴᴇɴ ɢʀᴀᴅᴜᴀᴛᴇᴅ from the University of California, Santa Barbara with high honors in pre-law in 1976. It was during his "junior year abroad" in 1974 while turning 21 in France, that he discovered life beyond tacos. After graduation, a one month stay in both Burgundy and Champagne convinced him to attempt a career in wine rather than continue on to law school.

Beginning with the 1978 harvest, Jim Clendenen was assistant winemaker at Zaca Mesa Winery for three vintages, a valued training experience. In 1981 his vision broadened with three harvests in one year as Jim worked crush and directed the harvest at wineries in Australia and France. Three harvests in one year confirmed his masochistic tendencies.

In 1982 Clendenen decided, along with now ex-partner Adam Tolmach, to start his own winery in leased quarters. Au Bon Climat (which means "a well exposed vineyard") has grown to over 30,000 cases through careful reinvestment from its own production.

The winery has cultivated an international reputation for its Pinot Noir, Chardonnay, and Pinot Blanc. Au Bon Climat is frequently recognized as one of the best wineries in the world by such notable writers as Robert Parker, Oz Clark, Dan Berger and Matt Kramer. In 2001 *Food & Wine* named Jim "Winemaker of the Year," in 2004 *Wine & Spirits* named Jim Clendenen one of the world's "50 Most Influential Winemakers" and *Wein Gourmet*, Germany's leading wine magazine, named him "Winemaker of the World."

AU BON CLIMAT

Jɪᴍ Cʟᴇɴᴅᴇɴᴇɴ, Oᴡɴᴇʀ

P O BOX 113

LOS OLIVOS, CA 93441

805.937.9801

WWW.AUBONCLIMAT.COM

Dungeness Crab Salad

Bourride

Bronzini à la Provençale

Grand Café Banana Cream Pie

Grand Café

GRAND CAFÉ
FABRICE ROUX,
EXECUTIVE CHEF

501 GEARY

SAN FRANCISCO, CA 94102

415.292.0101

WWW.GRANDCAFE-SF.COM

YOU CAN'T HELP BUT BE AWESTRUCK ENTERING GRAND CAFÉ, THE French restaurant located adjacent to the Hotel Monaco two blocks from Union Square and close to San Francisco's Theater District. Inspired by La Coupole on Boulevard du Montparnasse, it is, by anyone's standard, GRAND. You enter a world of 30-foot high pillars, molded ceilings, art deco chandeliers, and bronze sculptures by renowned artist Albert Guibara. It takes your breath away.

One of the first buildings reconstructed after the earthquake of 1904, Grand Café was the site of live theatre and still shows signs of its origins in its expansive dining floor, the bar situated at the original stage and the spectacular mezzanine. Add to that the comfortably elegant seating, the 'eternity' mirrors and the original artwork and you have a setting that indulges your senses as the menu indulges your palate.

Grand Café's Executive Chef Fabrice Roux creates memorable fare as he reinterprets French brasserie-style cuisine. His Vanilla and Rum Infused Foie Gras au Torchon with Mango-Pineapple Chutney is a delightful blend of flavors that teases your tongue with its rich flavor accented by the delicate sweetness of the chutney. Chef Roux's Grand Cassoulet with Duck Confit, Baby Back Ribs and Turkey Artichoke Sausage is just one of his piece d'resistance entrées that will have you coming back for more.

Grand Café also offers a pre-fixe menu perfect for a light meal before or after the theater. Cap off your evening with a slice of Grand Banana Cream Pie and a night at the luxurious Hotel Monaco and you have San Francisco at its best.

Dungeness Crab Salad

1/2 LB DUNGENESS CRAB MEAT   SERVES 4
2 BUNCHES CHIVES, DICED

❖ SALAD

1/3 LB CELERY ROOT
1/2 GRANNY SMITH APPLE
2 RUBY RED GRAPEFRUIT
1/3 CUP MAYONNAISE
SALT AND PEPPER

❖ LEMON DRESSING

1 CUP CORN SYRUP
1 CUP RICE VINEGAR
3 CUPS EXTRA VIRGIN OLIVE OIL
2 MEYER LEMONS

❖ Make a julienne of celery root and apple and combine with 1/3 cup of mayonnaise. Set aside. Peel and segment the grapefruit to use as a garnish.

❖ Combine corn syrup, rice wine vinegar and lemon together in a blender. Slowly add extra virgin olive oil to mixture to create dressing. Pass in a chinois.

In a bowl, combine half of the diced chives, crabmeat and 1/3 cup dressing.

ASSEMBLY

Place julienned celery root and apples in a circle in the center of the plate. Fan segmented grapefruit around the julienned items. Place crabmeat on top. Garnish with diced chives.

68

Bourride

❖ BROTH   SERVES 6

1 ONION
1 CARROT
1 FENNEL
1 14 OZ CAN WHOLE TOMATO
1 SPRIG THYME
1 BAY LEAF
1 SPRIG BASIL
4 TBSP EXTRA VIRGIN OLIVE OIL
3 CUPS WHITE WINE (CHARDONNAY)
1 1/2 QT FISH STOCK
1 PINCH SAFFRON
1 TSP SPANISH SMOKE PAPRIKA
1 CLOVE GARLIC
SALT AND PEPPER

❖ AIOLI

1 CLOVE GARLIC
1 CUP EXTRA VIRGIN OLIVE OIL
1 LEMON
SALT AND PEPPER

❖ Peel and cut the carrots, fennel and onions mirepoix size. In large saucepan, pour 4 tbsp extra virgin olive oil. Add the vegetables. Smash a clove of garlic. Add garlic to the vegetables and sauté without color for 2 minutes. Deglaze with the Chardonnay. Add the whole tomato, fish stock, bay leaf, thyme and 1 sprig of basil. Season with salt and pepper, saffron and the Spanish smoke paprika. Simmer for 45 minutes. Pass in a chinois and reserve.

❖ Put the 2 egg yolks in a bowl. Add the garlic clove. Whisk lightly with the cup of extra virgin olive oil to obtain a mayonnaise-like emulsion. Finish with a squeeze of lemon juice. Season with salt and pepper.

❖ Toast baguette dice in extra virgin olive oil with 1 chopped clove of garlic. Make sure not to burn the garlic, it will give it a bitter taste.

✤ Put the bourride in a blender. Slowly start to incorporate the aioli. Pass in a chinois. You will get a smooth broth. Warm the soup. Add the fish and shrimp. Let it simmer for 3 to 4 minutes. Don't boil it because the broth will separate "like broken mayonnaise." Put a few croutons in each soup bowl. Pour the smooth soup on top. Chiffonade the remaining basil sprig and use for garnish.

✤ **CROUTONS**

1/4 SOURDOUGH BAGUETTE, 1'' DICE OR STORE BOUGHT GARLIC CROUTONS

4 TBSP EXTRA VIRGIN OLIVE OIL

1 CLOVE GARLIC, CHOPPED

✤ **SOUP**

4 OZ WHITE FISH, ROCK COD, TILAPIA OR PETRALE SOLE

6 SHRIMP, SIZE 16/20

BROTH

AIOLI

CROUTONS

1 SPRIG OF BASIL FOR GARNISH

69

Bronzini à la Provençale

SERVES 6

✤ In a medium saucepan of boiling water, blanch the basil leaves for exactly 1 minute. Using a wire skimmer, transfer the basil leaves to a bowl of ice water. Drain and dry the leaves on paper towels. In a blender, combine the basil and olive oil. Blend on high speed until smooth. Season with salt and pepper.

✤ With a vegetable peeler, peel the red and yellow peppers. Seed the peppers and cut into julienne (2" long and 1/8" thick). Cut the onion into julienne. In a small saucepan, heat the olive oil over low heat until fragrant. Add the peppers, onion, coriander, cumin, salt and pepper. Cook, stirring occasionally, until the mixture has the consistency of marmalade, about 25 to 30 minutes. Set aside and keep warm.

✤ **BASIL OIL**

1 BUNCH BASIL LEAVES

1/2 CUP EXTRA-VIRGIN OLIVE OIL

SALT AND FRESHLY GROUND PEPPER

✤ **PEPPER CONFIT**

2 RED BELL PEPPERS

1 YELLOW BELL PEPPER

1 CUP EXTRA VIRGIN OLIVE OIL

1 LARGE SWEET WHITE ONION (SUCH AS MAUI)

PINCH OF GROUND CORIANDER

PINCH OF GROUND CUMIN

SALT AND FRESHLY GROUND BLACK PEPPER

❖ COUCOUS

2 CUPS COUSCOUS

1 1/4 CUP LOW-SALT CHICKEN BROTH

SALT AND FRESHLY GROUND PEPPER

❖ Put the couscous in a large bowl. In a small saucepan, bring the chicken broth to a boil. Pour the broth over the couscous. Stir in the salt and pepper. Cover with plastic wrap. Let stand for 10 minutes.

❖ FISH

1 TBSP EXTRA VIRGIN OLIVE OIL

SALT AND FRESHLY GROUND PEPPER

6 6 OZ BRONZINI FILETS (FRENCH SEA BASS OR LOUP DE MER)

❖ In a large sauté pan or skillet, heat the olive oil over medium high heat. Season the filets on both sides with salt and pepper. Add to the pan, skin side down, and reduce the heat slightly. Cook for 3 to 4 minutes on the skin side only.

❖ GARNISH

2 TOMATOES, PEELED, SEEDED AND FINELY DICED

6 CURED BLACK OLIVES

6 TBSP EXTRA-VIRGIN OLIVE OIL

SALT AND FRESHLY GROUND PEPPER

6 FRESH BASIL LEAVES

❖ In a small bowl, combine the tomatoes, black olives, salt, pepper and 6 tbsp of olive oil. Stir well.

ASSEMBLY

To serve, stir the basil oil into the couscous. Mound in the center of warmed plates. Place the fish on top of the couscous. On the side of the couscous, place a quenelle of the pepper confit. Sprinkle the garnish around the plate. Place a basil leaf on top of each filet.

Grand Café Banana Cream Pie

❖ MACADAMIA NUT CRUST

1 LB 2 OZ FLOUR

8 OZ MACADAMIA NUTS

5 OZ SUGAR

1 1/2 TSP SALT

9 OZ BUTTER

2 EGG YOLKS

SERVES 6

❖ Lightly toast the macadamias at 350° for about 5 minutes. Be careful, macadamias will burn easily. Remove from oven. When cool, chop nuts in a food processor with 1/4 of the flour until the mixture is a fine meal. Remove the macadamias to a bowl. Stir in the rest of the flour. Cream the butter, sugar and salt together in a mixer with the paddle attachment until it is pale. Add the yolks and blend in. Add the flour mixture and blend until it comes together as dough. Chill for at least 30 minutes. Can be made 3 days ahead.

❖ Whisk the yolks, eggs, sugar and cornstarch together in a bowl until pale. Set aside. Scrape the vanilla bean into the milk. Bring to a boil. Pour 1/2 the milk mixture into the eggs while whisking. Bring the rest of the milk back to a boil over medium low heat. Add the egg mixture to it. Stir until the mixture simmers. Turn the heat to low and cook, while stirring, for 2 minutes. Remove from heat and pour into bowl. Stir in the banana schnapps. Put plastic wrap directly on top of the mixture or smear with butter to prevent skin from forming. Chill for at least 2 hours. Can be made up to 2 days in advance.

❖ Bring the coconut milk just to a simmer. Set aside and keep warm. Put the sugar and water in a 2 qt saucepot. Wash down the sides and put over medium heat. Allow the sugar to cook until it is a golden brown. Turn off the heat. Add the warm coconut milk while stirring. (Be careful, the caramel will bubble up while you add the coconut milk so wear oven mitts to protect your hands and wrists.) Strain the caramel sauce and cool down. If the sauce seems thin, simmer for about 10 minutes. Can be made up to 1 week ahead and refrigerated. Bring to room temperature before serving.

ASSEMBLY

Roll the shortbread dough out on a piece of parchment paper to 1/4" thick, using some flour to keep it from sticking. It is a buttery dough so if it starts to get too warm to work with, chill it for 5 minutes, then continue. Cut the dough into 4 1/2" circles and line the tart molds. Chill for 30 minutes. Bake at 325° for approximately 20 minutes or until the shells are golden brown. Cool and remove the shells from the molds. Shells can be made the day before serving.

Toast the coconut in the oven at 325° for approximately 15 minutes. Make sure to stir every 5 minutes so it browns evenly. It should be golden brown when it is done. Allow to cool. Set aside.

Whip the cream, sugar and banana schnapps to soft peak. Set aside.

Whisk the pastry cream until it softens. Fill the shells 3/4 full. Slice the bananas into 1/2" thick disks and arrange 4 pieces in each shell.

Fill the rest with the whipped cream. Smooth off the top with a warm spatula. Cover the top with the toasted coconut. Chill until ready to serve. Can be assembled up to 5 hours ahead.

To serve, make a small pool of the caramel coconut sauce. Place the Banana Cream Pie in the middle and drizzle more sauce on top. The sauce is sweet so adjust the amount to personal taste. Sprinkle the toasted macadamias around the plate and serve. Enjoy!

❖ BANANA PASTRY CREAM

10 OZ MILK
1/2 VANILLA BEAN
2 EGG YOLKS
1 1/2 OZ CORNSTARCH
3 1/2 OZ SUGAR
1 OZ BUTTER (OPTIONAL)
1 OZ BANANA SCHNAPPS LIQUOR (SUCH AS 99 BANANAS)

❖ CARAMEL COCONUT SAUCE

8 OZ SUGAR
4 OZ WATER
4 OZ UNSWEETENED COCONUT MILK

ASSEMBLY

6 INDIVIDUAL TART MOLDS, 3 1/2" IN DIAMETER
4 RIPE BANANAS
7 OZ WHIPPING CREAM
1 OZ SUGAR
1/2 OZ BANANA SCHNAPPS
2 OZ MACADAMIA NUTS, TOASTED AND ROUGHLY CHOPPED
8 OZ LARGE FLAKE SWEETENED COCONUT

71

Wine Pairing

DUNGENESS CRAB SALAD
EDNA VALLEY VINEYARD PINOT GRIS,
PARAGON VINEYARD

BOURRIDE
EDNA VALLEY VINEYARD CHARDONNAY,
PARAGON VINEYARD

BRONZINI À LA PROVENÇALE
EDNA VALLEY VINEYARD SAUVIGNON BLANC,
PARAGON VINEYARD

GRAND CAFÉ BANANA CREAM PIE
EDNA VALLEY VINEYARD SWEET EDNA,
CENTRAL COAST

72

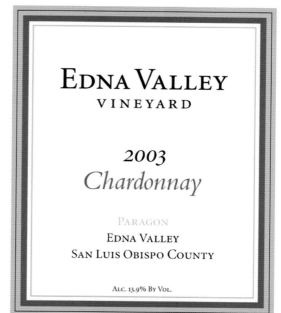

EDNA VALLEY

VINEYARD

2003
Chardonnay

PARAGON
EDNA VALLEY
SAN LUIS OBISPO COUNTY

ALC. 13.9% BY VOL.

SINCE OUR FIRST VINTAGE IN 1980, we have been pioneers in making fine wines from the Edna Valley appellation, which is noted for its distinctive volcanic and sedimentary soils. One of the first wineries in San Luis Obispo County, Edna Valley Vineyard is a partnership between Diageo North America and the Niven family.

Located just five miles from the Pacific Ocean, Edna Valley Vineyard is blessed with one of the longest and coolest growing seasons in California. As a result, the grapes have time to develop wonderful fruit flavors while retaining sufficient acidity to make them refreshing.

Classic Burgundian techniques are the core of our minimalist approach to winemaking. We handle the grapes gently and use imported French oak barrels for fermentation and aging with minimal pumping, fining and filtration. Our Chardonnay and Pinot Noir have repeatedly been chosen as favorites among popular publications such as the *New York Times* and *Bon Appetit*.

Visitors to Edna Valley Vineyard can enjoy our latest releases in a tasting room rated "Best Wine Tasting Room" in San Luis Obispo County. We offer something for everyone in the family. You can sample great wines, take a tour of the underground cellar, or shop for unique items at the gift shop. Bring a picnic and you can dine on the patio with a spectacular view of the vineyard and sweeping views of the valley. Our award–winning hospitality center is perfect for private events. The event center also plays host to several events open to the public such as cooking classes and winemaker dinners.

EDNA VALLEY
VINEYARD

THE NIVEN FAMILY,
OWNER
DIAGEO NORTH AMERICA,
OWNER

2585 BIDDLE RANCH ROAD

SAN LUIS OBISPO, CA 93401

805.544.5855

WWW.EDNAVALLEY.COM

Harris' Steak Tartare

Baby Spinach Salad with Soy Dressing

Harris' Petit Filet Pepper Steak

Fresh Fruit Tart

Harris' Restaurant

HARRIS RESTAURANT
GOETZ BOJE,
OWNER
MICHAEL BUHAGIAR,
EXECUTIVE CHEF

2100 VAN NESS
SAN FRANCISCO, CA 94109
415.673.1888
WWW.HARRISRESTAURANT.COM

FOR NEARLY A CENTURY, THE LANDMARK ADDRESS OF 2100 VAN NESS AVENUE has hosted some of the finest meals on the West Coast. When Harris' Restaurant opened its doors at the location in 1984, it continued the rich tradition of luxurious dining in a comfortable, sophisticated setting. *Gourmet Magazine* and *Wine Spectator* ranked Harris' as one of the nation's Top 10 steakhouses.

Accompanying the world-renowned beef, chicken and seafood dishes are an array of imaginative and tasty appetizers, side dishes, salads, and desserts and one of the 'worlds' greatest wine lists created by Jonathan Tennenbaum. Following the meal, Harris' offers a dessert list of homemade pastries and ice creams, crème brûlée and cheesecake.

Harris' wine list reflects the elegance and charm of the restaurant itself. The wine list focuses on California wines, but also offers many selections from wine growers around the world. There are over 20 selections offered by the glass and an array of late-harvest dessert wines.

To a passerby, Harris' is a handsome restaurant located on a busily traveled corner of San Francisco. There is a famous display window in front of the restaurant, which houses large cuts of aged beef. Harris' features four different dining rooms and a large Chicago, Brunswick-style mahogany bar. The main dining room offers curved, plush booths, high ceilings, brass chandeliers, and a skylight, which softens a lush mural by local artist Barnaby Conrad of a bucolic scene along the King's River in Central California.

Simply put, Harris' sets the stage for the quintessential steakhouse experience.

Harris' Steak Tartare

4 OZ GROUND FILET MIGNON
1 TSP RED ONION, FINELY CHOPPED
1 TSP PARSLEY, CHOPPED
1/2 TSP RED WINE VINEGAR
1/2 TSP SALT
1/4 TSP FRESH GROUND BLACK PEPPER
3 DASHES TOBASCO SAUCE
3 DASHES WORCESTERSHIRE SAUCE
1/3 TSP DIJON MUSTARD
1 TSP APPLE CIDER DRESSING

✤ TOAST ROUNDS
1 THIN FRENCH BAGUETTE,
SLICED AT A SLIGHT ANGLE.
OLIVE OIL

✤ APPLE CIDER
VINAIGRETTE
1 WHOLE EGG
1 2/3 CUP CANOLA OIL
1/3 CUP LEMON JUICE
1/3 CUP APPLE CIDER VINEGAR
1 TSP WORCESTERSHIRE SAUCE
1/2 TSP DIJON MUSTARD
1 CLOVE GARLIC, CRUSHED
1 TSP SUGAR
SALT AND PEPPER

SERVES 2

Combine all ingredients with a fork. Do not overmix. Serve with toast rounds.

✤ Lay sliced baguette rounds out on a baking sheet and dab with olive oil. Lightly toast in oven to a very pale golden brown. Let cool to room temperature.

✤ Whisk vigorously to emulsify. Salt and pepper to taste.

76

*Baby Spinach Salad
with a Soy Dressing*

SERVES 2

1/2 LB BABY SPINACH, WASHED

1/4 CUP MUSHROOMS, SLICED

1/4 CUP APPLE WOOD SMOKED BACON, CHOPPED

12 CHERRY TOMATOES

1/8 CUP SOY DRESSING

2 TBSP TOASTED PINE NUTS

❖ Mix dressing ingredients together in a small bowl.

Place the spinach in a separate bowl. Add dressing and mushrooms. Mix lightly. Place on chilled plate. Top with bacon, pine nuts and tomatoes.

❖ SOY DRESSING

4 TBSP SALAD OIL

1 TBSP SOY SAUCE

1 TBSP SUGAR

1 TBSP RED WINE VINEGAR

Harris' Petit Filet Pepper Steak

1/8 CUP CLARIFIED BUTTER
2 8 OZ PETIT FILETS
1/8 CUP BRANDY
1/4 CUP BEEF STOCK
1/4 CUP HEAVY CREAM
SALT AND PEPPER TO TASTE

SERVES 2

Heat butter in skillet. Place seasoned filets in skillet for 2 minutes on each side for medium rare. Remove from pan. Add brandy and flame. Cook until flame dies. Add beef stock and cream. Reduce to half volume. Adjust seasoning. Pour over steaks and serve.

Fresh Fruit Tart

1 PINT FRESH STRAWBERRIES
6 KIWIS
1 PINT RASPBERRIES

SERVES 2

❖ Preheat oven to 350°.

❖ SWEET NUT TART CRUST
2 OZ PECANS, WALNUTS OR ALMONDS
1 3/4 OZ GRANULATED SUGAR
5 OZ FLOUR
1/8 TSP SALT
4 OZ UNSALTED BUTTER
1 LARGE EGG YOLK
2 TBSP HEAVY CREAM
1/2 TSP VANILLA EXTRACT

Finely chop nuts. Add sugar, flour and salt. Mix together. Add butter. Mix until completely combined. Add remaining ingredients and mix well. Dough should have a cookie dough consistency. Place dough in plastic wrap, form into a disk, wrap completely and chill. Roll out on floured surface to fit 8" or 9" tart shell. You may also use 4" tart shells. Freeze tart shell before baking. Bake until golden brown, about 10 or 12 minutes. Cool before filling with pastry cream.

❖ In a medium size, heavy bottom saucepan, bring milk and vanilla beans to a boil. (Avoid aluminum, as it will turn pastry cream gray.) In a mixing bowl, combine cornstarch, sugar and salt. Whisk. When milk has come to a boil, add roughly 1/3 of it to the egg mixture, whisking immediately. Add warmed egg mixture to remaining milk in saucepan. Place over medium heat, stirring constantly with a heat resistant spatula to avoid scorching. Once it begins to thicken, switch to a whisk and whisk constantly until it bubbles. Continue to whisk for 1 minute until the cornstarch has cooked out. Remove from heat and strain through a fine mesh cheesecloth. Stir in butter and vanilla extract until smooth. Place plastic wrap directly over the custard. Chill completely before filling the tart shell.

✤ In a saucepan, bring 1 quart of water to a boil. Place zest in a strainer in boiling water for about 15 seconds. Remove and place in iced water to stop the cooking process and retain color. Combine 1/2 cup sugar and 1/2 cup water and bring to a boil. Turn off heat and let cool to room temperature.

Toss blanched zest in the water/sugar syrup. Lay out on a sheet tray lined with parchment paper. Sprinkle with granulated sugar. Bake until crispy. While still hot, cover the entire top with granulated sugar. Once cooled, remove zest from sugar. Store in an airtight container.

ASSEMBLY

Fill tart shells 3/4 of the way up with pastry cream. Smooth the top with a spatula. Slice strawberries and kiwi 1/4" thick. Arrange in a fan-like pattern, alternating strawberries and kiwi. Leave center for the raspberries. (You may glaze with an apricot glaze to give it a shine.) Sprinkle candied zest around tart. Serve.

✤ PASTRY CREAM
2 CUPS WHOLE MILK
1/2 HALF VANILLA BEAN
1 1/4 OZ CORNSTARCH
4 OZ SUGAR
PINCH OF SALT
2 WHOLE EGGS
1 1/2 OZ UNSALTED BUTTER
1/2 TSP VANILLA EXTRACT

✤ CANDIED CITRUS ZEST
3 EACH LEMONS, ZESTED
3 EACH LIMES, ZESTED
2 EACH ORANGES, ZESTED
1/2 CUP SUGAR
1/2 CUP WATER
APRICOT GLAZE (OPTIONAL)

79

Wine Pairing

Harris Steak Tartare
2002 Grgich Hills Zinfandel
Napa Valley

Baby Spinach Salad with Soy Dressing
2004 Grgich Hills Fumé Blanc
Napa Valley

Petit Filet Pepper Steak
2001 Grgich Hills Cabernet Sauvignon
Napa Valley

Fresh Fruit Tart
2002 Grgich Hills "Violetta"
Napa Valley

80

GRGICH HILLS

Napa Valley
CABERNET SAUVIGNON
2001

PRODUCED AND BOTTLED BY
GRGICH HILLS CELLAR, RUTHERFORD, CA

LOCATED IN THE HEART of Napa Valley, Grgich Hills Cellar was founded in 1977 by Miljenko "Mike" Grgich and Austin Hills of the Hills Bros. Coffee family. Mike Grgich's 1973 Chateau Montelena Chardonnay had just won the now-famous Paris Tasting, besting the top white Burgundies and creating high demand for Grgich Hills' wines from the start. There, in a now-historic blind tasting, a panel of eminent French judges swirled, sniffed and sipped an array of the fabled White Burgundies of France and a small sampling of upstart Chardonnays from the Napa Valley. When their scores were tallied, the French judges were shocked—they had chosen Mike's Chardonnay as the finest white wine in the world. Mon Dieu!

Grgich Hills' philosophy of consistency, quality and longevity has led to ongoing critical and consumer acclaim. Our balanced and food-friendly wines—Chardonnay, Cabernet Sauvignon, Merlot, Zinfandel, Fumé Blanc and botrytis-affected *Violetta*—are world-renowned for their elegance and finesse. Since the 2003 vintage, all of our wines are estate grown with the fruit from our five Napa Valley vineyards. Because great wines begin in the vineyard, we now farm our 366 acres biodynamically and organically.

The quality of the fruit, the tender care in the winery and the aging regimen make Grigich Hills' handcrafted wines immediately enjoyable on release as well as capable of maturing gracefully. As winemaker Mike Grgich likes to say, "We treat our six different wines like special children, and we pour all of our love, attention and artistry into nourishing their exceptional character and flavor."

GRGICH HILLS CELLAR

MILJENKO "MIKE" GRGICH AND AUSTIN HILLS, OWNERS

1829 ST. HELENA HIGHWAY

P O BOX 450

RUTHERFORD, CA 94573

800.532.3057

WWW.GRGICH.COM

Crisp Shaved Potatoes Flash Fried with Herbs and Vinegar

Prawns Brochette with Spicy Vinaigrette

Stuffed Bell Pepper with Portabella Mushrooms and Machego Cheese

Piperade

Beret Basque Mousse with Chocolate Sprinkles

Iluna Basque

ILUNA BASQUE
MATTIN NOBLIA,
CHEF

701 UNION STREET

SAN FRANCISCO, CA 94133

415.402.0011

www.ilunabasque.com

ILUNA BASQUE, OR BASQUE NIGHT, CONJURES THE FEEL, THE AROMA, and the taste of the Basque countryside. Legend has it that a Basque aubergiste laid a thin slice of Serrano ham on a glass plate of cider. Some say this was to enhance the flavor of the ham; others say it was to keep the flies away. Either way it began what is known today as the delicacy of tapas. Tapas have become a delightful way of enjoying more selections by serving small portions.

Founder and Executive Chef Mattin Noblia began his career as a 14 year-old under the tutelage of noted chef Dominique Jolie. After receiving his "chef de cuisine" diploma, he began his culinary journey in restaurants in France and Switzerland, eventually landing him in San Francisco and his own restaurant, Iluna Basque. His inspiration comes from the unique way various foods can be assembled to create a savory dish.

"Iluna Basque serves authentic home-cooked Basque food in a charming, hip atmosphere. Mattin Noblia is one of the freshest talents to hit San Francisco in a very long time." (Susan Dyer Reynolds, *NorthSide*)

The warm ambience of Iluna Basque in the North Beach area gives credence to the adage "good food, good wine, good night." All three combine to bring you an evening that includes palate pleasing tapas such as Piccilos Peppers Stuffed with Spanish Salt Cod "Bacalao"; Amaxti Style Duck Rilette with Roasted Croustinis; Spanish Tortilla with Baby Spinach and Goat Cheese; and Beret Basque Chocolate Mousse served with a full bodied wine. When dining at Iluna Basque, why have one entrée when you can enjoy several?

Crisp Shaved Potatoes Flash Fried with Herbs and Vinegar

6 MEDIUM TO LARGE POTATOES
4 GARDEN HERBS
(THYME, ROSEMARY, SAGE, BASIL)
OIL OR FAT FOR DEEP-FRYING
VINEGAR
SALT

SERVES 4

Wash and peel the potatoes. Slice very thin with a mandoline. An old-fashioned cabbage slicer can be used (careful of the fingers) or use a sharp knife or food processor with a thin slicing blade. Put the slices immediately into a bowl of cold water. Let stand for at least 1 hour. Dry well by shaking them in a towel.

In 390° oil, fry the herbs first. Set aside. Then fry the potatoes until a light golden brown, one layer at a time. Do not fry too many at once. Pat dry with absorbent paper. Leave the tail and head shells intact. Salt lightly. Top with the herbs and a splash of vinegar. Enjoy them warm.

Prawns Brochette with Spicy Vinaigrette

1 LB KING SIZED PRAWNS, UNCOOKED
3 SHALLOTS, CHOPPED
1/4 CUP EXTRA VIRGIN OLIVE OIL
1/4 CUP RED WINE VINEGAR
1/2 TSP CHILE POWDER
1 TSP PAPRIKA
1 TSP GRATED FRESH GINGER (OPTIONAL)
2 CLOVES GARLIC, CRUSHED
SALT AND PEPPER TO TASTE
10 SKEWERS
3 TBSP CHIVES, CHOPPED (OPTIONAL)

SERVES 4-5 AS A MAIN COURSE OR 10 AS TAPAS

In a small saucepan, add 1/4 cup of olive oil and shallots. Bring to a boil. Stir in the vinegar. Add paprika, ginger, garlic and chile. Set aside.

Wash the prawns. Pat dry with absorbent paper, leaving tail shells intact. Thread onto skewers, 3 or 4 per skewer.

Grill the prawn skewers in a lightly oiled and very hot pan. Place them in a dish and drizzle the sauce on top. Sprinkle with chopped chives to garnish.

Stuffed Bell Pepper with Portabella Mushrooms and Manchego Cheese

SERVES 4

1 TBSP EXTRA-VIRGIN OLIVE OIL

8 OZ PORTABELLA MUSHROOMS, DICED

1 ONION, DICED

1 GARLIC CLOVE, CRUSHED

4 BELL PEPPERS OF ANY COLOR

2 FRESH TOMATOES, DICED

1/2 CUP SHAVED MANCHEGO CHEESE

SALT AND FRESH GROUND PEPPER

3 TBSP CHIVES, CHOPPED (OPTIONAL)

Preheat oven to 350°.

Heat the olive oil in a saucepan. Add the onion, garlic and mushrooms. Cook gently for 3 minutes, stirring occasionally. Stir in the tomatoes. Simmer, uncovered, for 10 to 15 minutes, stirring occasionally. Remove from the heat. Stir in salt and pepper to taste.

Cut the peppers in half lengthwise and seed. Blanch in a pan of boiling water for about 3 minutes. Drain. Place the peppers in a shallow oven-proof dish. Pour olive oil on top of the peppers. Bake for 20 minutes. Fill with the vegetable mixture. Sprinkle each pepper with shaved Manchego cheese. Bake for another 5 to 10 minutes or until the cheese is melted and bubbling. Garnish with chopped chives and serve.

Piperade

8 RED BELL PEPPERS,
SEEDED AND FINELY SLICED
1 ONION, FINELY SLICED
6 GARLIC CLOVES, CRUSHED
6 BIG TOMATOES, CHOPPED
1 TSP SUGAR
1/4 CUP EXTRA-VIRGIN OLIVE OIL
1/8 TSP PIMENT D'ESPELETTE
(BASQUE GROUND PEPPER)
SALT AND FRESHLY GROUND PEPPER
1 BAY LEAF
4 OR 6 EGGS
2 SLICES SERANO HAM PER DISH
VINEGAR

Heat pan over medium–high heat. Add the olive oil. Add the bell peppers, onions and garlic. Sauté until it begins to render out some of its water. Add tomatoes, sugar, piment d'espeltte and bay leaves. Check the seasoning. Add salt and pepper to taste. Cook for about 30 minutes, stirring occasionally. Remove the bay leaf. Fry the Serano slices lightly. Poach the eggs in boiling water with a splash of vinegar. Serve the Piperade in a cazuela with the ham and the egg on top.

86

Beret Basque Mousse with Chocolate Sprinkles

SERVES 6

Melt the chocolate in the top of a double broiler (or bain marie) over low heat. Stir in the coffee. Cool to room temperature. Whip the cream until thick, gradually adding the sugar until stiff peaks form. Fold the chocolate mixture into the whipped cream. Pour into 6 individual serving glasses. Refrigerate the mousse for at least 2 hours before serving. Serve with chocolate sprinkles and strawberries on top (optional).

1/2 POUND SEMISWEET OR BITTERSWEET DARK CHOCOLATE
2 TSP BREWED COFFEE (OPTIONAL)
5 CUPS HEAVY CREAM
1/4 CUP SUGAR
1/2 CUP CHOCOLATE SPRINKLES
1/2 CUP STRAWBERRIES, QUARTERED AND SLICED THIN (OPTIONAL)

Crisp Shaved Potatoes Flash Fried with Herbs and Vinegar
2002 Mina Ranch Chalk Hill Chardonnay

Prawns Brochette with Spicy Vinaigrette
2003 Diamond Oaks Carneros Pinot Noir

Stuffed Bell Pepper with Portabella Mushrooms
and Machego Cheese
2002 Diamond Oaks Hira Ranch Merlot

Piperade
2002 Diamond Oaks Silver Carneros Merlot

Beret Basque Mousse
with Chocolate Sprinkles
2003 Diamond Oaks Alexander Valley Cabernet Sauvignon

88

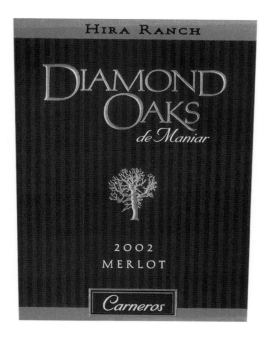

DIAMOND OAKS
WINERY

DINESH MANIAR,
OWNER

1595 OAKVILLE GRADE

OAKVILLE, CA 94562

707.948.3000

WWW.DIAMOND-OAKS.COM

"EXCELLENCE TAKES TIME" IS THE MANTRA OF DINESH MANIAR, owner of Diamond Oaks Winery. Like the ancient oaks that inspired the name, Diamond Oaks Winery stands as a testimony to patience.

It was the purchase of fifty-seven acres of Diamond Mountain in 1977 that started Dinesh and his family on a twenty-seven year journey that would ultimately lead to the creation of Diamond Oaks Winery. Planned initially as a family retreat to escape the stresses of the city, the Calistoga property became an entrepreneurial endeavor when the Maniars began cultivating and selling grapes. The dream of owning a winery was born.

With five hundred and fifty acres of meticulous vineyards within four regions— Carneros, Alexander Valley, Chalk Hill, and Napa Valley—Maniar grapes are highly sought after by the country's most prestigious wineries. With each acquisition, new knowledge was gained in the Maniar's quest to produce grapes of the highest quality.

After more than twenty years of honing their skill and reputation as growers of premium grapes, the Maniars were ready for the next step. In Fall 2000, the family made the first Diamond Oaks wines.

"It takes great grapes to make great wine," says Dinesh. "You can't do it any other way. My approach to winemaking is like that of a diamond cutter. I only want to cut and polish the stone in a way that will best illuminate its natural brilliance—so it is with our wines."

Arugula Salad with Fennel, Page Mandarin, Apple and Pomegranates with a Lemon Vinaigrette

Leek and Potato Soup with Seared Scallops

Potato Wrapped Bluenose Seabass

Flourless Chocolate Cake

ISA
LUKE SUNG,
CHEF

3324 STEINER STREET
SAN FRANCISCO, CA 94123
415.567.9588

NOT MANY CHEFS HAVE THEIR OWN RESTAURANTS BY AGE 26, BUT CHEF Luke Sung is never one to take things slowly. Named after his daughter Isabelle, Isa Restaurant opened in the Marina District in the summer of 2000. It has been hailed as the hot place to go in San Francisco and lauded by the *San Francisco Chronicle*, which wrote, "On every count—food, service, and atmosphere—Isa should be as hard to get into as the French Laundry."

Relax as you spend a San Francisco evening sitting in Isa's main dining room which spills out onto the sidewalk, or enjoy the romantic garden setting of the restaurant's bi-level back patio with its heated lamps and flowery garden. Isa offers cuisine with a twist—French tapas meets California cool.

The knowledgeable and friendly wait staff will walk you through the dozen or so small plates that make up Isa's interesting menu. Begin with the mouth watering Seared Foie Gras with Rhubarb and Strawberries and a Balsamic Reduction. The Ragout of Veal Sweetbreads and Wild Mushrooms with Potato Galette and the Potato Wrapped Sea Bass with Brown Butter and Capers will leave you wanting to further explore Isa's French style small plate servings.

Chef Sung creates the type of combinations one can eat every day. To further prove the point, he opened Lux Restaurant, his latest endeavor featuring Asian-French small plate servings.

Arugula Salad with Fennel, Page Mandarin, Apple and Pomegranates with a Lemon Vinaigrette

4 CUPS OF ARUGULA (I PREFER YOUNG
ARUGULA THAT IS NOT
BITTER OR BRUISED)
1 PIECE OF FENNEL BULB, 1/8" SLICE
2 PIECES OF SIERRA BEAUTY OR FUJI
APPLES, CUT INTO MATCHSTICK SIZE
4 PIECES PAGE MANDARIN, PEELED AND
SLICED INTO 3 THICK SLICES
1/2 CUP POMEGRANATE SEEDS

❧ VINAIGRETTE

1 CUP LEMON JUICE, FRESHLY SQUEEZED
1 TSP LEMON ZEST
1 TSP SHALLOTS, FINELY MINCED
2 CUPS EXTRA VIRGIN OLIVE OIL
(I LIKE FRUIT FORWARD, PEPPERY, COLD
PRESSED OR GREEN OLIVE OIL)
2 PINCHES OF SALT
FRESHLY GROUND PEPPER
1 PINCH OF SUGAR

SERVES 4

❧ Mix all together to emulsify.

ASSEMBLY

Combine arugula, fennel and apple in a mixing bowl. Add vinaigrette to taste. Divide the salad onto 4 separate plates. Scatter the mandarin over the salad. Sprinkle with pomegranate seeds. Serve quickly so that the arugula holds its firmness.

Leek and Potato Soup with Seared Scallops

SERVES 4

In medium size, non-reactive, heavy bottom, stainless steel soup pot, sweat leeks with 1 1/2 tbsp olive oil. Cook until leeks soften. Stir as you add chopped potatoes and bouquet garni. Right before all the moisture evaporates from the pot, add chicken stock and the water. Bring to a boil on medium heat. Blend and pass it through with a pasoir.

Boil it again. Add herbs, cream and salt and pepper to taste. In a sauté pan, sear scallops, turn only once when there is a nice crust with a perfect bronze color. Salt and pepper to taste. Pour the soup into 4 serving bowls. Add scallops. Drizzle extra virgin olive oil lightly on top. Serve hot.

4 CUPS LEEKS, WHITE PART ONLY,
CUT IN HALF LENGTHWISE, SLICED THIN
2 MEDIUM RUSSET POTATOES,
PEELED AND CHOPPED
BOUQUET GARNI
1 STALK CELERY
2 SPRIGS THYME
2 BAY LEAVES
SMALL HANDFUL ITALIAN PARSLEY STEMS
2 TBSP OF BUTTER
3 TBSP EXTRA VIRGIN OLIVE OIL
2 TBSP PARSLEY, CHOPPED
1 TSP FRESH TARRAGON, CHOPPED
4 CUPS CHICKEN STOCK
4 CUPS WATER
4 TBSP CREAM
12 SCALLOPS
SALT AND PEPPER

Potato Wrapped Bluenose Seabass

1 1/2 LBS SEABASS
2 LARGE RUSSET POTATOES
4 TBSP BUTTER
1 TBSP CAPERS, LIGHTLY CHOPPED
2 TBSP TOMATOES, DICED
2 TBSP LEMON JUICE
1 TBSP PARSLEY, CHOPPED
1 TBSP FRESNO CHILIES, SLICED AND SEEDED
4 TBSP OLIVE OIL.

SERVES 4

Preheat oven to 400°.

Skin and clean seabass. Cut into 4 portions of 4 1/2 oz each. Peel and very thinly slice the potatoes lengthwise using a mandolin, if available. In a pot of boiling water, blanch the potatoes for about 30 seconds. Plunge the slices in a cold-water bath. Place on paper towels to dry. Season the fish with salt and pepper. Wrap the potato slices tightly around the fish, making sure they overlap. In a nonstick skillet, heat the olive oil. Place the fish in the skillet and sear on all sides. Place the fish in the oven to finish cooking for 2 to 4 minutes, depending on the thickness. Check doneness by inserting a knife in the center part of the fish. Feel the "warm" temperature on your lips. Take the fish out of the pan and let rest. Remove the extra fat in the skillet and wipe clean with a towel.

In the same pan, heat butter to brown. Add capers, peppers, salt and pepper, lemon juice and parsley. Place the fish on a serving plate and pour the butter sauce over it.

94

Flourless Chocolate Cake

SERVES 8   BUTTER FOR PAN COATING
POWDERED SUGAR FOR PAN DUSTING
7 EGGS
9 OZ BITTER SWEET CHOCOLATE
(60% COCOA BUTTER)
4 OZ BUTTER
4 OZ SUGAR
1 ORANGE, ZEST AND JUICE
1 SPLASH GRAND MARNIER

Preheat oven to 325°.

Separate eggs. Keep egg whites room temperature in an electric mixer bowl. Keep the egg yolks in a bowl large enough for all of the batter.

In a nonstick 8" round by 3" tall cake pan, lightly coat with butter and dust with powdered sugar. Combine chocolate and butter in a stainless steel mixing bowl. Set the bowl over simmering water to melt.

Attach wire whisk to mixer. Mix the egg whites on low speed, slowly increase it to high speed while adding half the sugar to triple its volume. Mix approximately 5 minutes.

In the bowl with the yolks, whisk together the other half of the sugar until ribbon-like. Add chocolate and butter mixture. Mix well.

This is the most important part for this cake to properly rise—carefully fold the egg whites into the chocolate mixture. Add zest, juice and Grand Marnier.

Bake the cake in the oven for approximately 40 minutes. Check the center of the cake with a small knife. When the knife comes out clean, it is done. Let the cake sit for 2 minutes inversed on a cooling rack. Unmold from the cake pan.

95

Wine Pairing

Arugula Salad with Fennel,
Page Mandarin, Apple and Pomegranates
with a Lemon Vinaigrette
2003 Morgan Sauvignon Blanc Monterey

Leek and Potato Soup with Seared Scallops
2003 Morgan Chardonnay Monterey

Potato Wrapped Bluenose Seabass
2003 Morgan Twelve Clones Pinot Noir

Flourless Chocolate Cake
2002 Morgan Syrah Monterey

MORGAN

Chardonnay   2003
                                Monterey

MORGAN
WINERY

DAN AND DONNA LEE,
OWNERS

590 BRUNKEN AVENUE

SALINAS, CA 93901

831.751.7777

WWW.MORGANWINERY.COM

IN 1982, AFTER WORKING IN THE WINE INDUSTRY AND IN BANKING, Dan Morgan Lee and his wife Donna started Morgan Winery. In the Fall of 1996, their dream of buying a property for growing their own grapes and providing a building site for their permanent winery came true. The 65-acre property in the northern end of the Santa Lucia Highlands was perfect for growing Pinot Noir and Chardonnay, the two cornerstone wines of Morgan Winery.

The Santa Lucia Highlands appellation of Monterey, from which Morgan Winery sources most of its Chardonnay and Pinot Noir fruit, is one of the finest in California for Burgundian varietals. The combination of cool temperatures, significant winds and low rainfall stress the vines to the point where the typical growing season is four to five weeks longer than most California wine regions. The result is mature and intense flavors—apple and pear in Chardonnay, black cherry in Pinot Noir, fresh cut lime in Pinot Gris and a spicy blackberry note in Syrah.

Morgan Winery utilizes other Monterey appellations, such as the Arroyo Seco, for its rich Chardonnay component. The warmer southern Monterey appellations are the source for the intense, racy Sauvignon Blanc character and for a powerful, structural aspect to the Syrah bottlings.

Morgan Winery's estate vineyard, the Double L, is farmed organically. It is the only organic vineyard in the Santa Lucia Highlands. The micronutrients and microbes that leach into the water are beneficial to the vines and result in more colorful and flavor-intensive fruit. A blind taste test revealed that the lots that received the treatment had more detailed fruit expression, better structure and better aroma. Better wine, hands down, and part of the reason Dan Lee was *San Francisco Chronicle*'s 2003 Winemaker of the Year.

Liberty Duck Liver Flan Crème Caramel with Apple Caviar and Sherry Vinegar Caramel

Autumn Pumpkin Soup

Red Wine Braised Oxtails

Organic Red Indian Carrot Cake

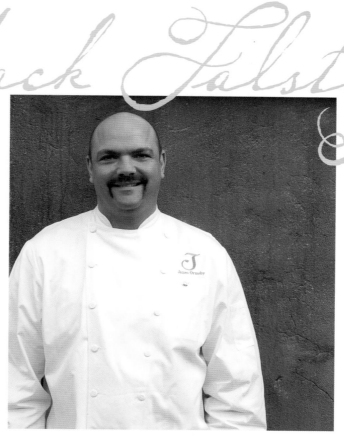

JAMES ORMSBY,
EXECUTIVE CHEF
GILLIAN BALLANCE,
WINE DIRECTOR

598 SECOND STREET

SAN FRANCISCO, CA 94107

415.836.9239

WWW.PLUMPJACK.COM

THE NEWEST IN THE LINE OF SUCCESSFUL PLUMPJACK BUSINESSES, Jack Falstaff brings culinary life to the SOMA neighborhood near SBC Park. Comfortable and cozy with plenty of windows and wood paneling, the walls and pillars are covered in sensuous green suede, the same fabric that covers the chairs and banquettes in the dining room. Jack Falstaff also offers spacious outdoor seating on the heated patio. The restaurant is perfect for accommodating Giants fans with indoor or outdoor lunch or dinner before and after Giants games.

PlumpJack's award winning Executive Chef James Ormsby has created an imaginative American menu at Jack Falstaff with his "slow food" and organic approach to cooking. Think of slow roasted pork roast (10 hours) or Atkins ranch lamb top sirloin, braised cabbage and buckwheat blinis to get your mouth watering. But unlike most restaurants of this caliber, the dishes don't contain refined flour or starches. This bodes well for the diner wanting a full and healthy meal. Ormsby's skill in the kitchen has been featured in *Food & Wine*, *Food Arts*, *San Francisco Chronicle* and *San Francisco Examiner*.

To remain true to the healthy style of the cuisine, the wine list at Jack Falstaff features many wine producers who are "getting back to the land" either through organic or biodynamic viticulture. The results are wines of unadulterated purity that speak of the place from which they came—perfect as an accompaniment to the fresh local food served at Jack Falstaff. In recognition of Wine Director Gillian Ballance's wine selection, *Food & Wine* recently awarded Jack Falstaff "Best New Wine List."

Liberty Duck Liver Flan Crème Caramel with Apple Caviar and Sherry Vinegar Caramel

❧ DUCK LIVER FLAN

SERVES 6

1/2 CUP FRESH DUCK LIVER
(CHICKEN LIVER OR FOIE GRAS
CAN BE USED AS A SUBSTITUTE)
1 CUP HALF AND HALF
3 EGG YOLKS
1 TBSP BUTTER
PINCH FRESH GROUND NUTMEG
2 TBSP DRY SHERRY
SALT AND PEPPER

❧ Heat the butter in a non-stick pan. Season livers with salt and pepper. Cook until medium rare, about 2 to 3 minutes. Deglaze with sherry. Add half and half, nutmeg and the egg yolks. Purée in a blender until smooth. Strain the mixture through a fine strainer to remove skim and foam off the top. Taste for seasoning and add salt if needed.

❧ CARAMEL

1/2 CUP SUGAR
1/2 CUP WATER

❧ Mix sugar and water in a small pot. Cook over high heat until golden brown. Pour into 6 custard cups. Jostle cups to evenly distribute caramel inside the cups. Let cool. Divide the custard mixture into the cups. Put in a pan. Add water to the pan halfway up the height of the cups. Cover with foil. Bake at 300° until set (about 45 minutes). Let cool.

❧ APPLE CAVIAR

2 GRANNY SMITH APPLES
2 TBSP SUGAR
1 TBSP APPLE CIDER VINEGAR
PINCH OF SALT

2 TSP SHERRY VINEGAR
6 CUSTARD CUPS FOR SERVING

❧ Peel the apples. Thinly slice and dice into a very fine brunoise. Take the apple scraps and grate with a cheese grater. Place grated scraps in a clean muslin cloth and squeeze to get the juice. Pour juice, sugar and vinegar over apple dice. Add apple dice to a non-stick pan. Cook over medium heat until apples are tender and the liquid has been absorbed. Season with a pinch of salt. Put mixture in a container and keep at room temp or refrigerate.

When ready to serve, remove the custards from the molds by using a knife to separate around the sides of the cups. Some caramel juices will come out so un-mold onto a large plate and drain off the syrup. Save the syrup. Add 2 tsp of sherry vinegar to the syrup. Strain and reserve.

ASSEMBLY

In a shallow bowl, place the custards carefully in the center. Spoon the caramel syrup and sherry vinegar mixture over the top. Garnish with the apple caviar. Serve with walnut bread.

Autumn Pumpkin Soup

SERVES 6

101

Over medium heat in a large heavy bottom pot, heat butter until golden. Add the thyme, sage and onion. Stir until the onions are lightly golden. Add the sherry. Toss in the pumpkin cubes and honey. Cook for 5 minutes. Add the water, cinnamon and nutmeg. Cover and gently boil for 10 minutes or until the pumpkin is tender. Add the canned pumpkin and cook for an additional 5 minutes. Add the cream, salt, pepper and lime juice. Process this mixture in a blender in batches. Strain through a fine sieve as you go. Place the soup in a tureen. Season to taste with salt and pepper.

❖ Garnish with toasted pumpkin seeds, drizzled pumpkin seed oil, crème fraiche and chopped chives.

4 CUPS SUGAR PUMPKIN,
PEELED AND CUBED

1 15 OZ CAN PUMPKIN

1/4 LB UNSALTED BUTTER

1/4 CUP WHITE ONION, DICED

2 TSP FRESH THYME LEAVES

2 TSP FRESH SAGE, CHOPPED

2 TBSP HONEY

1/4 CUP DRY SHERRY

5 CUPS WATER

2-3 TBSP SALT

1 TSP GROUND CINNAMON

1 TSP GROUND NUTMEG

GROUND BLACK PEPPER TO TASTE

1 CUP HEAVY CREAM

1 TBSP FRESH LIME JUICE

❖ GARNISH

PUMPKIN SEEDS, TOASTED

PUMPKIN SEED OIL

CRÈME FRAICHE

CHIVES, CHOPPED

Red Wine Braised Oxtails

❖ OXTAILS

SERVES 4

4 LBS OXTAILS, CUT AT JOINTS
SALT AND PEPPER
1 BOTTLE (750 ML) CABERNET
SAUVIGNON OR OTHER DRY RED WINE
3 CUPS FAT-SKIMMED BEEF BROTH
1/4 CUP BALSAMIC VINEGAR
1 TBSP FRESH ROSEMARY LEAVES,
CHOPPED (OR 1 TSP DRIED ROSEMARY)
1 TBSP FRESH TARRAGON, CHOPPED
(OR 1 TSP DRIED TARRAGON)
1 TBSP FRESH THYME LEAVES, CHOPPED
(OR 1 TSP DRIED THYME)
YUKON GOLD MASHED POTATOES
CARAMELIZED ROOT VEGETABLES
1 1/2 TBSP CORNSTARCH
FRESH THYME SPRIGS, RINSED

❖ YUKON GOLD MASHED POTATOES

2 LBS YUKON GOLD OR
RUSSET POTATOES
3/4 CUP MILK OR HALF AND HALF
2 TBSP BUTTER OR MARGARINE
SALT AND PEPPER

❖ CARAMELIZED ROOT VEGETABLES

2 CARROTS OR 12 BABY CARROTS
1 6 OZ PARSNIP OR 12 BABY PARSNIPS
1 8 OZ TURNIP
1 LB PEARL ONIONS OR 12 CIPOLLINI
ONIONS OR 10 OZ FROZEN
PEARL ONIONS, THAWED
1 1/2 TBSP OLIVE OIL
1 TBSP FRESH THYME LEAVES, CHOPPED
SALT AND PEPPER TO TASTE

❖ Preheat oven to 450°.

Rinse oxtails and pat dry. Trim off and discard excess fat. Sprinkle lightly all over with salt and pepper. Place in a 12" x 17" roasting pan. Bake in oven, uncovered, turning once with tongs until oxtails are well browned all over (30 to 40 minutes total).

Add wine, broth, 1/4 cup vinegar, rosemary, tarragon and thyme to pan. Gently stir to mix and scrape browned bits free. Cover pan tightly with foil.

Return to 325° oven until meat is very tender when pierced, about 2 1/2 hours.

Skim and discard any fat from braising liquid. Boil uncovered over high heat, stirring often until reduced to 3 cups, about 14 minutes. In a small bowl, mix cornstarch with 2 tbsp of water until smooth. Stir into braising liquid until mixture boils and thickens. Taste and add 1 to 2 more tsp vinegar, if needed.

❖ Peel potatoes. Cut into 2" chunks. Combine potatoes and about 1 quart water in a 3 to 4 quart pan. Cover and bring to a boil over high heat. Reduce heat and simmer until potatoes mash very easily, about 20 minutes. Drain potatoes and return to pan. Set aside.

Warm milk and butter in a microwave-safe container in a microwave oven at full power until just steaming (or warm in a saucepan over medium heat on the stove top). Add milk mixture to potatoes and mash with an electric mixer on medium speed or a potato masher until smooth. Season to taste with salt and pepper. Cover and keep warm in a 200° oven until ready to use.

❖ Preheat oven to 450°.

Peel carrots. Cut carrots and parsnip crosswise into 1/2" thick slices. Dice turnip into 1/3" dice. (If using baby vegetables, leave whole.)

In a 9" x 13" pan, mix vegetables with olive oil and thyme. Sprinkle lightly with pepper. Bake in oven, turning vegetables occasionally with a wide spatula, until well browned and tender when pierced (about 30 minutes). Add salt to taste. Serve warm or at room temperature.

ASSEMBLY

Mound Yukon Gold mashed potatoes equally in the centers of 4 wide, shallow

102

bowls. With tongs, lift oxtails from braising liquid and arrange around mashed potatoes. Scatter caramelized vegetables over meat. Cover loosely with foil and keep warm in a 200° oven.

Ladle sauce over meat and caramelized vegetables. Garnish with thyme sprigs. Add salt and pepper to taste.

Organic Red Indian Carrot Cake

SERVES 8

Preheat oven to 350°.

Grease a 9" x 3" deep cake pan and line the bottom with parchment paper. Combine the flour, sugars, salt, cinnamon, baking powder and baking soda into a bowl. Stir until well blended. Combine the carrots, eggs, oil and vanilla in a large bowl. Whisk well. Whisk in the pineapple and walnuts. Add the dry ingredients to the liquid ingredients. Stir just to blend.

Pour the batter into the prepared cake pan. Bake in the center of the oven for 55 to 60 minutes, until the top feels firm and a toothpick inserted in the center comes out clean. Cool in the pan on a rack. Remove cake from the pan. Dust the top with sifted powdered sugar just before serving. (A cream cheese frosting can be used or a dollop of whipped cream.)

1 CUP WHOLE WHEAT PASTRY FLOUR
1/2 CUP GRANULATED SUGAR
1/2 CUP BROWN SUGAR
1 TSP SALT
1 TSP CINNAMON
1 TSP BAKING POWDER
3/4 TSP BAKING SODA
1 1/2 CUPS ORGANIC RED CARROTS, PEELED AND GRATED (ORANGE CARROTS CAN BE USED AS A SUBSTITUTE)
4 LARGE EGGS
1/2 CUP CANOLA OIL
2 TSP PURE VANILLA
1 CUP (8 OZ) CANNED CRUSHED PINEAPPLE IN JUICE (NOT HEAVY SYRUP)
1/2 CUP TOASTED WALNUTS, CHOPPED
POWDERED SUGAR

104

LIBERTY DUCK LIVER FLAN CRÈME CARAMEL
WITH APPLE CAVIAR AND SHERRY VINEGAR CARAMEL
2003 DRY SELECT GEWURZTRAMINER (RRV)

AUTUMN PUMPKIN SOUP
2003 MARTINELLI ROAD CHARDONNAY

RED WINE BRAISED OXTAILS
2003 GIUSEPPE & LUISA ZINFANDEL

ORGANIC RED INDIAN CARROT CAKE
2003 JACKASS HILL MUSCAT
ALEXANDRIA

THE MARTINELLI FAMILY HAS BEEN FARMING IN SONOMA COUNTY since 1860. We began by raising sheep, cattle, potatoes, walnuts, prunes, apples and wine grapes. The ancient apple orchards and vineyards, along with new vineyard plantings, are the family's prevailing crops. The lofty view on top of the Jackass Hill Vineyard has not changed much since 1899 when Giuseppe and Luisa Martinelli planted the first vines there. The original centurion houses and barns are still in use by the family.

All of the Martinelli wines are produced from estate grown grapes farmed by Lee Martinelli Sr. and sons Lee Jr. and George, continuing five generations of the proud family legacy of caretaking the land. Martinelli Winery produces small lots of wine from our outstanding single vineyards. In the creation process, we work from beginning to end with our winemaker Helen Turley and viticulturist John Wetlaufer; analyzing soil samples; choosing root stocks, varietals, and clones that are best matched to a particular growing site; pruning the fields each season; and blending the fruit for the finished wines. Each of our vineyards is thinned to yield between one to three tons of fruit per acre. At harvest time, the grapes are hand selected according to taste and fermented with wild yeast in small French oak barrels.

Our guests can sample Martinelli wine in our historic hop barn, which has maintained its authentic turn-of-the-century atmosphere. Here we feature our estate wines along with a wide selection of gourmet foods produced locally in Sonoma County.

MARTINELLI
WINERY

THE MARTINELLI FAMILY,
OWNERS

3360 RIVER ROAD

WINDSOR, CA 95492

707.525.0570

WWW.MARTINELLIWINERY.COM

QUAIL LOLLIPOPS

CRAB NAPOLEON

BUTTER POACHED LOBSTER AND AUTUMN VEGETABLES IN A BAKED MINI PUMPKIN

COCONUT TAPIOCA WITH PASSION FRUIT SORBET

La Folie

LA FOLIE
ROLAND PASSOT,
CHEF

2316 POLK STREET

SAN FRANCISCO, CA 94109

415.776.5577

WWW.LAFOLIE.COM

LA FOLIE IS A CHARMING FAMILY RUN RESTAURANT WITH A DÉCOR THAT emanates New York chic and sophistication. You enter a room of polished strips of reddish-copper moabi wood and a large floating frame of pearly Venetian plaster hanging from the ceiling. Rich copper-brown drapes cover the opening to the kitchen.

Chef Roland Passot serves generous portions of astoundingly good food. "Passot earned national status early in his career as a protégé of Jean Banchet, the renowned owner of Le Francais near Chicago, and as the chef of the glamorous French Room in Dallas. He returned to San Francisco and in 1988 opened La Folie." Michael Bauer, *San Francisco Chronicle*

You simply can't err when you order from Passot's exuberant but disciplined menu. It changes often, but memorable starters have included wonderful foie gras plates and unforgettable lobster salad with spicy mango vinaigrette. Recent main courses have included a roti of quail and squab stuffed with wild mushrooms and wrapped in crispy potato strings, and tournedos of roasted salmon served with a purée of sweet onions and Pinot Noir sauce. Enjoy the "Discovery" tasting menu to sample as many dishes as you choose. To accommodate the growing number of vegetarians, Passot has thoughtfully included a separate Vegetable Lover's Menu.

The owner's French roots surface in the decidedly Franco-California wine list. Choose from an extensive selection of excellent reds or opt for one of the "discovery wines" from lesser known wine regions of Australia and Chile.

A La Folie, le client est roi!

Quail Lollipops

3 BONELESS QUAIL
1 FOIE GRAS (GRADE A),
ROOM TEMPERATURE
1 TBSP SALT
1 TSP BLACK PEPPER
6 TO 8 WHOLE GARLIC CLOVES
1/2 CUP WHITE WINE
3 SPRIGS THYME
1/2 CUP ROASTED CHICKEN STOCK
(JUS DE POULET)

❖ CANNELLONI
3/4 LB MUSHROOMS: CHANTERELLES,
YELLOW AND BLACK, CHOPPED OR
JULIENNE (OR ANY OTHER
MUSHROOMS AVAILABLE)
1 TBSP BUTTER
1 TBSP CLARIFIED BUTTER OR OLIVE OIL
1 CLOVE GARLIC, CHOPPED
2 TBSP CHIVES, CHOPPED
2 LEEKS, WHITE PART ONLY

SERVES 4

Preheat oven to 400°. Remove the upper wing tip and thigh bones from the quail, leaving the drumsticks and lower wing bones. Check the breasts for cartilage and remove. Split in half lengthwise. Set aside.

Cut foie gras into 6 pieces, 3/4" thick by 3" long. Season with salt and pepper. Stuff each half quail with foie gras. Place the foie gras between the breast and thigh meat and wrap the quail around the foie gras, skin side out. Refrigerate for 1 hour. Tie with twine to maintain shape. Quail half should be elongated with wing bone at one end and drumstick at the opposite end.

In 2 medium sauté pans over medium heat, place quail in clarified butter or olive oil, breast sides down. Roast on all the sides. Add the garlic cloves. Place pans in preheated oven for 5 minutes. Remove from oven and set breasts aside. Crush whole cooked garlic cloves with fork or spoon. Degrease and deglaze the sauté pans with white wine. Add stock and reduce to half. Add fresh thyme for 2 minutes and strain. Reserve.

❖ In sauté pan over medium high heat, melt fresh butter. Add mushrooms. Sauté for 3 to 4 minutes. Mix well. Add salt and pepper, fresh garlic and chopped chives (last). Set aside.

Cut white part of leek 4" long. Make an incision lengthwise, 3 to 4 layers deep. Blanch leeks in boiling salted water for 3 minutes. Quickly place in ice bath and pat dry with paper towel. Lay blanched leek flat. Fill with 2 tbsp of sautéed mushroom mixture. Roll tightly, keeping mixture 1/2" from each end of cannelloni. To reheat, sauté over medium heat with olive oil and 2 tbsp of butter.

ASSEMBLY

Cut each lollipop into 3 equal pieces. Place on rectangular plate with drumstick piece on left side, standing bone end up; boneless center cut in the middle; and wing piece on the right side, bone end up. Drizzle pan sauce an each lollipop. Place 1 cannelloni at the 12 o'clock position above the quail pieces. Serve.

Crab Napoleon

SERVES 4

✤ Combine juice, Muscat, cinnamon and star anise in medium saucepan. Bring to a boil. Remove from heat and strain into clean bowl. Set aside.

In a separate bowl and while above ingredients boil, soften gelatin sheets in cold water. Remove excess water by squeezing and draining sheets. Add to hot juice mixture. Stir until completely dissolved. Set aside to cool. On chilled plate, add gelée mixture from 1/8" to 1/4" thick. Place plates in refrigerator to set. (Quick tip: Cut a wine cork into 4 equal size discs and place on rim of plate. Stack a new plate on corks. Do as many as needed.)

✤ Slice pineapple 1/8" thick. Place on very lightly greased silpat or expopat. Place in oven at 200° or less. Cook until golden brown and crisp. Carefully remove using an offset spatula. Reserve between dry paper towels.

ASSEMBLY

While gelée sets, mix together first 7 ingredients for crab salad. In separate bowl, mix next 5 ingredients. Sprinkle dressing on frisee.

Once gelée has set, place a generous portion of crab mixture on a plate and top with a pineapple chip. For the next layer, place a smaller portion of crab mixture and frisee, then top with a chip. For the final layer, place a large pinch of crab mixture and frisee, then top with a final chip. Place 1 piece of crab meat and more frisee on top of the final chip. Garnish by placing chive onto the frisee.

1 CUP PICKED DUNGENESS CRAB MEAT, RESERVE 2 LUMP PIECES FOR GARNISH

1 TBSP ROMA TOMATO, PEELED, SEEDED AND DICED

1 TBSP TARRAGON, CHOPPED

1 TBSP CHIVES, CHOPPED

1 TBSP GRANNY SMITH APPLE, DICED

1 TBSP CUCUMBER, PEELED, SEEDED AND DICED

3/4 TBSP LEMON JUICE

1 1/2 TBSP EXTRA VIRGIN OLIVE OIL

1 TSP LIME ZEST

1 TSP LEMON ZEST

1/4 TSP SALT

3 GRINDS BLACK PEPPER

1 HEAD FRISEE LETTUCE, WASHED AND CUT IN HALF

2 CHIVE STEMS

✤ APPLE GELÉE

1 CUP APPLE JUICE

1 CUP MUSCAT

1 STICK CINNAMON

3 STAR ANISE

4 GELATIN SHEETS

✤ PINEAPPLE CHIPS

1 PINEAPPLE

NON-STICK SPRAY

Butter Poached Lobster and Autumn Vegetables in a Baked Mini Pumpkin

SERVES 4 ✤ POACHED LOBSTER

3 1 1/2 LB LOBSTERS, FEMALE IF POSSIBLE

1 CARROT, PEELED AND DICED

1 ONION, PEELED AND QUARTERED

1/2 BUNCH CELERY, WASHED AND CUT

1 TBSP ANISE SEED

1 TBSP FENNEL SEED

✤ In a wide bottom pot filled with water, add carrots, onion, celery, all the spices and vinegar. Bring to a boil. Place lobsters in the pot and cook 5 minutes. Remove lobsters and immediately place in an ice bath to stop further cooking.

Lay lobsters on a towel. Pull legs off, snap off knuckles. Remove thin part of claw and bone inside the claw meat by twisting and pulling out. Lay claw

(continued)

1 TBSP CORIANDER SEED
1 TBSP BAY LEAF
1 TBSP GROUND CAYENNE PEPPER
1/2 CUP RED WINE VINEGAR

✤ BABY PUMPKINS
4 BABY PUMPKINS

✤ MIXED VEGETABLES
8 BABY LONG CARROTS,
CLEANED AND PEELED
12 HARICOT VERTS, CLEANED
4 BABY TURNIPS,
CLEANED AND PEELED
8 PEARL ONIONS, CLEANED AND
OUTER SKIN REMOVED
8 YELLOW WAX BEANS, CLEANED
8 ASPARAGUS TIPS, CLEANED
8 ENGLISH PEAS OR
SNAP PEAS, SHELLED
8 FAVA BEANS, SHELLED
2 TBSP EXTRA VIRGIN OLIVE OIL
1/4 CUP PURIFIED WATER
1 PINCH SUGAR
SALT AND PEPPER

*If any of the vegetables are out of season,
use your imagination for substitutes.*

✤ BEURRE FONDUE
3 TBSP SHALLOTS, MINCED
2 TBSP OLIVE OIL
1 CUP DRY WHITE WINE
1 TBSP ANISE SEED
1 TBSP FENNEL SEED
2 STAR ANISE
1 FRENCH CAYENNE PEPPER
1 TBSP CORIANDER
1 BUNCH FRESH TARRAGON
1 1/2 TO 2 LB BUTTER
1 BAY LEAF
SALT AND PEPPER

GARNISH
TARRAGON
CHERVIL
CHIVE BATTON

flat on a towel and cover. Gently pound with a wide mallet or heel of a knife. Use your fingers to gently push the meat through the large opening at the other end. Lay the tail meat flat and cut in half lengthwise through the middle. Remove the vein running through the inside of the tail. Reserve meat on a paper towel, cover and refrigerate.

For the knuckles, cut off the top joint of each knuckle. Use scissors to cut away the shell along the smooth outside edge of the knuckle. Use your finger to open up the shell and remove the meat.

For the body shell, pull back and discard the sack behind the head. Reserve the roe (dark green color), body and legs for for sauce or stocks in freezer bags. Discard tomalley and lungs.

✤ Preheat oven to 400°. Place whole baby pumpkins in baking dish with 1" of water. Cover with foil and cook for 30 to 45 minutes or until tender. Remove from oven and cool. Once cool, cut out top of pumpkin and save for later. Using a small spoon or melon baller, remove the inside flesh of the pumpkin and discard. Keep pumpkins and tops at room temperature.

✤ Individually blanch all vegetables in boiling water. Remove to ice bath. Set aside until ready to heat. Just before serving, heat sauté pan over medium heat. Add olive oil, water and sugar. Then add root vegetables, carrots, turnips and onions. As root vegetables start to heat, add beans and asparagus. Add peas and favas last. Do not overheat or vegetables will lose color. Once heated, skim from pan with slotted spoon and fill pumpkins with equal amount of vegetables (1 carrot, 2 onions, 2 wax beans, etc.).

✤ In saucepan over medium heat, add olive oil. Add shallots and sauté for a few minutes until translucent. Add all spices. Sauté for a few more minutes and add white wine. Bring to a boil for 2 minutes. Add butter and whisk consistently to obtain an emulsify "Beurre Fondue." Strain out shallots and add fresh tarragon. Set aside.

ASSEMBLY

Heat Beurre Fondue over low heat. Do not overheat or sauce will break. Remove from heat source. Add lobster to warm for 2 to 3 minutes.

Place vegetable-filled pumpkin on each plate and top with warm lobster (1 claw and 1/2 tail per plate). Place pumpkin tops at an angle on the side of the pumpkins. Drizzle Beurre Fondue over lobster. Garnish with tarragon, chervil and chive batton.

Coconut Tapioca with Passion Fruit Sorbet

SERVES 6-8

❧ In a bowl, mix sugar, lemon juice, corn syrup and passion fruit–mango pulp. Churn in sorbet machine for 15 to 20 minutes, depending on machine. Reserve in stainless steel container in freezer. If there is no access to a sorbet machine, many specialty food stores sell passion fruit and mango sorbets.

❧ Combine all the ingredients in a large saucepan. Let stand for 10 minutes. Place the pan over medium heat and bring the mixture to a boil. Lower heat and cook, stirring constantly to keep the mixture from sticking, 35 to 45 minutes or until pearls become translucent. Remove from heat and let cool.

❧ Preheat oven to 350°. In a robo-coupe or food processer with regular blade, mix eggs, sugar and coconut for 30 seconds. Slowly add melted butter until a paste is formed. Be careful not to overwork. Place in stainless steel bowl and let rest in refrigerator until solidified.

Using a silpat on a cookie sheet, space 1 tbsp of tuile batter every 4". With an offset spatula, spread the tuile mixture into circles approximately 3 1/2" in diameter.

Bake in oven for 8 minutes or until golden brown. Remove from oven and let rest on pan for 20 to 30 seconds. Carefully remove each tuile from pan. Place on cool flat surface and let harden. Once tuiles are hard, store in dry, covered container.

❧ Blanch the basil in salted boiling water for 60 seconds. Drain and transfer to an ice bath. Drain, squeeze dry and coarsely chop. Set aside.

In a deep, heavy saucepan with a candy thermometer attached, combine sugar, corn syrup and water. Heat over high heat to the soft-ball stage. The candy thermometer should register 235°.

Put basil in blender and pour hot syrup contents over basil. (Put lid on to blend then cover with kitchen towel. The heat will push the lid up and the towel prevents spillage.) Purée on low setting until smooth. (Be careful not to let contents overflow out of blender. It will be hot and can scald.) Strain through a fine-mesh sieve into a stainless steel bowl. Quickly place the bowl in an ice bath. Letting the heat stay on the basil will remove the bright green color. Pour into a plastic squirt bottle and refrigerate until ready to use.

To serve, pour 3/4 cup of the tapioca into a shallow soup bowl. Place a quenelle of sorbet on top. Drizzle a circle of basil syrup around the tapioca. Top with a coconut tuile and garnish with mint. Dust with confectioners sugar. Serve at once.

❧ PASSION FRUIT SORBET
1/4 QT MANGO PURÉE OR PULP
1/4 QT PASSION FRUIT PURÉE OR PULP
2 OZ SUGAR
1/2 LEMON, JUICED
1 TSP CORN SYRUP

❧ TAPIOCA
1 8 OZ PACKAGE (1 1/3 CUPS) SMALL PEARL TAPIOCA
4 CANS (54 FL OZ) UNSWEETENED COCONUT MILK
5 CUPS WHOLE MILK
1/3 CUP HONEY
3/4 CUPS SUGAR

❧ COCONUT TUILES
2 LARGE EGG WHITES
1/2 CUPS GRANULATED SUGAR
3/4 CUPS SHREDDED DRIED UNSWEETENED COCONUT
1/4 CUP UNSALTED BUTTER, MELTED

❧ BASIL SYRUP
1 BUNCH BASIL, STEMMED
1/2 CUP GRANULATED SUGAR
1/4 CUP CORN SYRUP
1/2 CUP WATER

CONFECTIONERS SUGAR FOR DUSTING
MINT SPRIGS FOR GARNISH

111

Wine Pairing

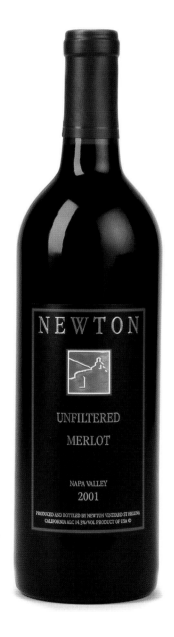

QUAIL LOLLIPOPS
2001 NEWTON UNFILTERED PINOT NOIR

CRAB NAPOLEON
2002 NEWTON UNFILTERED CHARDONNAY

BUTTER POACHED LOBSTER
AND AUTUMN VEGETABLES IN A BAKED MINI PUMPKIN
2001 NEWTON UNFILTERED MERLOT

COCONUT TAPIOCA WITH PASSION FRUIT SORBET
2003 CHARDONNAY RED LABEL

NEWTON

2002
UNFILTERED CHARDONNAY
NAPA VALLEY

Produced And Bottled By Newton Vineyard St Helena California, Alc 14.9%/Vol Product Of USA ©

NEWTON
VINEYARD

DR. SU HUA NEWTON,
OWNER

2555 MADRONA AVENUE

SAINT HELENA, CA 94574

707.963.9000

WWW.NEWTONVINEYARD.COM

SITUATED ON THE DRAMATIC SLOPES OF SPRING MOUNTAIN IN THE Napa Valley, Newton Winery's terraced vineyards, reminiscent of Chinese landscape paintings, reveal the origin of winemaker Dr. Su Hua Newton. The formal English *parterre* garden reflects the birthright of Peter Newton.

Peter and Su Hua Newton purchased one square mile of tumbling slopes high up on Spring Mountain overlooking St. Helena in 1977. The Estate was planted to Merlot, Cabernet Franc, Cabernet Sauvignon and Petit Verdot at elevations ranging from 500 to 1600 feet. Merlot thrives in a land that is rocky mixed with clay beneath the surface; Cabernet Franc and Petit Verdot like an impoverished soil; and Cabernet Sauvignon is happy in stony loam. The mountainous slopes of the vineyards not only have these soils, but also a full range of exposures. The elevation of Spring Mountain spares the vineyards from the drying heat on hot days, the vines get all the sunlight they need without any baking heat stress. Hillside vineyards are difficult to cultivate and are very labor intensive. However, the reward is richly flavored fruit.

Chardonnay needs chalky or loamy soil in a cooler region. Newton owns an old vineyard in Carneros and also has long-term grape contracts for several hillside vineyards verging on that region. Introduced in 1990, Newton Unfiltered Chardonnay is said to be the first unfiltered wine produced and sold in California, and is now regarded as an industry benchmark. All Newton wines are naturally fermented with the accent on the tastes of fruit.

Su Hua insists on picking only ripe grapes from the vine. Her method of quality control is to be involved in every aspect of the harvest, during which time she can be found daily among the pickers. To ensure that only ripe grapes are harvested, there can be up to four separate pickings in a single vineyard—very difficult to do but Su Hua believes there is no better way to produce a great wine.

Maytag Blue Cheese Soufflé

Bradley's Caesar Salad

Braised Colorado Lamb Shanks with Grits

Blackout Cake with Kumquat Chantilly Cream

Lark Creek Inn

THE LARK CREEK INN
MATT CHRISTIANSON,
CHEF

234 MAGNOLIA AVENUE

LARKSPUR, CA 94939

415.924.7766

WWW.LARKCREEK.COM

RESTAURATEURS BRADLEY AND JODY OGDEN AND MICHAEL AND LESLYE DELLAR have been drawing national media attention to The Lark Creek Inn since opening in 1989. Ogden, who helped redefine American cooking, could not have found a more ideal setting for his menus of new and old American classics than the picturesque Lark Creek Inn. Surrounded by towering redwoods, the sunny yellow house built in 1888 is a thorough delight from its entryway gardens to its stone floored sun porch. Out back, an umbrella shaded, and heat lamp warmed garden beside a meandering creek is the perfect spot for lunch, Sunday brunch or summertime dinner. A wood-burning brick oven is the focal point of the main dining room, where a glass ceiling lets the outdoors in.

Meals get off to a scrumptious start with a trio of house baked breads and salads made with the finest organic produce. Try the quintessential Caesar or such combinations as multi-colored homegrown tomatoes in balsamic vinaigrette with Buffalo mozzarella cheese. Expect such entrées on the daily changing menu as roasted pheasant with huckleberry sauce, toasted pearl pasta and grilled stone fruit; and grilled king salmon with saffron shellfish essence paired with truffled risotto cake and sugar snap peas. All-American desserts like warm chocolate brioche bread pudding with chocolate sauce and Chantilly cream are not to be missed. Luncheons feature such specialties as Southern fried chicken salad and crab cakes with tomato gazpacho. Many of the lunch items are also available at Sunday Brunch with the addition of traditional and not-so-traditional breakfast foods like fried sweetbreads and scrambled eggs and baked brioche French toast with wild berries and berry syrup.

The award winning wine list is both interesting and all-American. And values on both wine and food are excellent. For a quick bite or drink, the all-day menu and the chalkboard menu are offered on a walk-in basis in the bar and on the patio.

Maytag Blue Cheese Soufflé

❖ SOUFFLÉ SERVES 6 TO 8

4 EGGS, SEPARATED
8 OZ BLUE CHEESE
2 OZ BUTTER
2 OZ FLOUR
1 1/4 CUPS MILK
6-8 4 OZ RAMEKINS, BUTTERED AND FLOURED

❖ Melt butter and add flour to make a roux. Add milk and whisk until simmering. Cook out flour to make a béchamel. Crumble cheese into a bowl. Add hot béchamel to the bowl with the cheese.

As the mixture cools slightly, whip the egg whites to a medium peak. Add yolks to cheese mixture. Fold in egg whites. Portion into ramekins. Bake in a water bath at 300° until the eggs are set in the soufflés.

❖ SALAD

2 PINK LADY APPLES
2 CUPS ARUGULA
1 HEAD ENDIVE
24 WALNUTS
BLUE CHEESE FOR GARNISH
VINAIGRETTE

❖ To serve, slice apples and dress arugula and endive with a vinaigrette. Garnish with walnuts and blue cheese.

Bradley's Caesar Salad

SERVES 4

❧ Trim the romaine lettuce of any brown and bruised leaves. Tear the leaves into 2" pieces. Wash, dry and refrigerate.

Combine the garlic, capers and anchovies, mixing together to form a paste. Add the egg yolks, dry mustard, lemon juice, salt and 1/4 tsp of the pepper. Whisking continuously, very slowly add the olive oil. Continue whisking until all the oil has been added and the dressing is thick and smooth like mayonnaise. Refrigerate the dressing for 30 minutes so the full flavor can develop.

Place the romaine in a large bowl and add the remaining 1/2 tsp cracked black pepper. Pour the dressing down the sides of the bowl, lifting the lettuce up and over, coating the leaves evenly. Add the Parmesan croutons and toss. Place on plates and garnish with shaved Parmesan.

❧ Preheat oven to 350°.

Combine the garlic and butter in a small saucepan. Place over moderate heat until the butter has completely melted and is bubbling but not browning. Remove from heat and let stand for 15 minutes. Strain the butter and discard the garlic cloves.

In a bowl, toss the bread and butter, evenly coating the cubes. Place the bread cubes on a sheet pan and bake for 15 minutes. Stir them once or twice while baking.

Once the croutons have become deep golden brown and are crisp all the way through, remove them from the oven and place in a large bowl. Add the Parmesan cheese to the croutons while they are still warm. Toss the croutons and cheese together.

❧ SALAD

2 HEADS ROMAINE LETTUCE

2 LARGE CLOVES GARLIC, MINCED

1/2 TSP CAPERS, RINSED AND MINCED

6 ANCHOVY FILETS,
MASHED WITH A FORK

2 EGG YOLKS

1/4 TSP DRY MUSTARD

2 TBSP LEMON JUICE

1/4 TSP KOSHER SALT

3/4 TSP FRESH CRACKED PEPPER

1/2 CUP OLIVE OIL

PARMESAN CROUTONS (RECIPE BELOW)

1/2 CUP SHAVED PARMESAN

❧ PARMESAN CROUTONS

2 CUPS FRENCH BREAD,
CUT INTO 3/4" CUBES

6 SMALL GARLIC CLOVES,
PEELED AND CRUSHED

1/4 CUP UNSALTED BUTTER

1/2 CUP GRATED PARMESAN CHEESE

117

Braised Colorado Lamb Shanks with Grits

❖ SHANKS   SERVES 6

6 16 OZ COLORADO LAMB SHANKS

4 CARROTS, PEELED AND CHOPPED

4 STALKS CELERY, CHOPPED

4 WHITE ONIONS, PEELED AND CHOPPED

3 QTS BEEF OR VEAL JUS

1 BOTTLE RED WINE (CABERNET)

4 OZ CANOLA OIL

❖ Preheat oven to 350°.

Sear shanks in hot canola oil on the stovetop. When golden brown on all sides, remove from pan. Remove some of the fat from the pan and add vegetables. Brown the vegetables and deglaze with the red wine. Place vegetables in a braising pan, add the shanks and pour all the liquids over the vegetables and shanks. Bring to a simmer, cover and place in the preheated oven. Cook until a knife inserted along the bone is withdrawn easily.

❖ GRITS

1 CUP GRITS

1 ONION, DICED

2 TBSP CANOLA OR OLIVE OIL

2 CUPS WHOLE MILK

1 CUP CREAM

1 CUP VEGETABLE STOCK

4 TBSP UNSALTED BUTTER, SOFTENED

SALT AND PEPPER

❖ Combine the milk, cream and vegetable stock in a saucepot. Bring to a boil. Remove from heat and reserve. Heat the oil in a heavy-bottom pot. Add the onions. Cook over medium-low heat until translucent. Add the reserved liquid to the onions, then whisk in the grits. Turn the heat down to very low and cook until grits are softened (about 45 minutes to 1 hour) stirring frequently to avoid scorching. If the mixture becomes too thick, add more liquid. Stir in the butter and season with salt and pepper to taste. To serve, place the shanks on the grits and glaze with jus.

Blackout Cake with Chocolate Ganache and Kumquat Chantilly Cream

SERVES 6

CAKE

3 CUPS SUGAR

2 1/4 CUPS FLOUR

1 1/2 CUPS UNSWEETENED COCOA POWDER

1 1/2 TSP BAKING POWDER

2 1/4 TSP BAKING SODA

1 1/2 CUPS BUTTERMILK

4 LARGE EGGS

1/2 CUP COFFEE

3 OZ MELTED BUTTER

3 OZ CANOLA OIL

GANACHE

1 LB 8 OZ DARK CHOCOLATE, FINELY CHOPPED

4 OZ MILK CHOCOLATE, FINELY CHOPPED

1 CUP POWDERED COCOA, SIFTED

4 CUPS CREAM

1 CUP SUGAR

2 OZ SOFT BUTTER

KUMQUAT CHANTILLY CREAM

2 CUPS WHIPPING CREAM

1/3-1/2 CUP KUMQUAT SYRUP

3/4 CUP CANDIED KUMQUATS

KUMQUAT SYRUP

6 CUPS SUGAR

3 CUPS WATER

1/2 LEMON

VANILLA BEAN, SCRAPED

4 WHOLE CORIANDERS

3 CUPS KUMQUATS, SLICED AND WITH SEEDS REMOVED

✤ Preheat oven to 325°.

Butter a flat sheet pan. Sift first 5 ingredients 3 times. Combine next 3 ingredients and whisk into dry ingredients. Follow with butter and oil mixture. Pour batter into a sheet pan and bake for 10 to 15 minutes until set.

✤ Bring cream and sugar to a boil. Reduce heat to low and whisk in cocoa and chocolates. Remove from heat. Cool sauce by occasionally stirring. When lukewarm, stir in butter. Strain through a fine mesh sieve and allow to cool.

✤ Whip cream until slightly thickened. Slowly pour in syrup to taste. Continue whipping to medium peaks. Fold in kumquats.

✤ Combine first 5 ingredients and bring to a boil. Reduce heat and simmer for 8 to 10 minutes. Add sliced kumquats. Continue to simmer until kumquats are translucent, 10 to 12 minutes. Strain, reserving kumquats for Chantilly cream.

ASSEMBLY

Cut the sheet cake into thirds. Spread ganache onto each layer, placing 1/3 of the cake atop the ganache until you have a 3-layered cake. Thinly slice the cake lengthwise, as if slicing a loaf of bread. Place slice of cake on a plate. Add a dollop of the Kumquat Chantilly Cream.

119

Wine Pairing

Maytag Blue Cheese Soufflé
Iron Horse 2000 Brut Rose

Bradley's Caesar Salad
Iron Horse 2003 Cuvee R,
Sauvignon Blanc/Viognier Blend

Braised Colorado Lamb Shanks with Grits
Iron Horse 2002 Estate Pinot Noir

Blackout Cake with Kumquat Chantilly Cream
Iron Horse 2000 Russian Cuvee

120

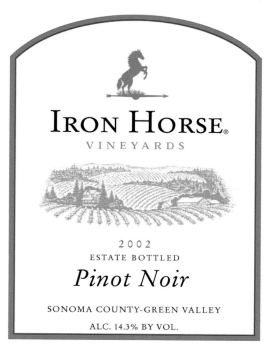

IRON HORSE
VINEYARDS

2002
ESTATE BOTTLED
Pinot Noir

SONOMA COUNTY-GREEN VALLEY
ALC. 14.3% BY VOL.

IRON HORSE IS NAMED AFTER a railroad stop located on the property at the turn of the century. Rodney Strong rediscovered it as a vineyard site and Forrest Tancer planted the original fifty-five acres of Chardonnay and fifty-five acres of Pinot Noir in 1970-1971. After searching for several years for a winery in Europe, Audrey and Barry Sterling happened upon Iron Horse in 1976, finding precisely what they had sought for so long.

Tancer and the Sterlings completely rehabilitated the vineyard, built the reservoir and installed the frost protection system. Built in 1876, the original Victorian structure on the property was restored and became the Sterling's home. The Iron Horse logo, the rampant horse on a weather vane, came from a 19th century weathervane found while clearing away the rubble during construction.

Iron Horse is best known for its Sparkling Wines. They have been served at the White House since 1985 beginning with the historic U.S.-Russian Summit meetings that helped to end the Cold War and continuing through the White House Millennium celebrations that ushered in the new century.

Iron Horse produces six prestige Cuvées. The current vintages are 1997 Blanc de Blancs, 1996 Brut LD (our *tête de cuvée*), 2000 Classic Vintage Brut, 2001 Wedding Cuvée (the bubbly for which we are best known), 2000 Brut Rosé and 2000 Russian Cuvée.

Pinot Noir is the winery's rising star. Iron Horse makes two bottlings—the Iron Horse Estate Pinot Noir and the limited production Thomas Road Pinot Noir. *Wine & Spirits*, *Bon Appetit* and *Quarterly Review of Wines* all ranked the 2001 Thomas Road as one of the top ten Pinot Noirs of the year. The next release of Thomas Road will be vintage 2004.

IRON HORSE
VINEYARDS

STERLING-TANCER FAMILY,
OWNER

9786 ROSS STATION ROAD

SEBASTOPOL CA 95472

707.887.1507

www.ironhorsevineyards.com

BEETS COLORIAGE

LOBSTER SALAD

BOUILLABAISSE PROVENÇALE

LEMON TART

La Suite

LA SUITE
JOCELYN BULOW,
OWNER
BRUNO CHEMEL,
EXECUTIVE CHEF

100 BRANNAN BTREET

SAN FRANCISCO, CA 94107

415.593.5900

WWW.LASUITESF.COM

RENOWNED RESTAURANTEUR JOCELYN BULOW'S RESTAURANT, LA SUITE, presents a true brasserie dining experience. Located in San Francisco's famous Embarcadero, La Suite is accompanied by sweeping views of the Bay Bridge.

The interior of the restaurant is a modern answer to Parisian *fin de siecle* brasseries. The sumptuous dining rooms feature dark wood columns and paneling accented with ochre colored walls and classic furniture. Nickel plated railings, a pressed tin ceiling, mirrors, stone tile floors, a zinc topped bar backlit with glowing amber and an open kitchen create a warm and inviting atmosphere. Art Deco crystal and glass chandeliers add sparkle. For dining *en plein air* there is a heated terrace.

The soul of La Suite is French, the service impeccable and the menu the creation of Chef de Cuisine Bruno Chemel. Chef Chemel began his professional career in Parisian restaurants after graduating from culinary academies in Moulins and Le Notre. You experience his expertise as you dine on Caramelized Cippolini Onion Tarte with Montrachet Cheese Creme Frâiche, Wood–Grilled Niman Ranch Entrecote aux Herbes de Provence with Bearnaise Sauce and Pomme Frites and Apple Tarte Tatin with Lavender Ice Cream.

French dining would not be complete without the cheese cart. It's an incredible array of European goat, cow and sheep milk cheeses.

"La Suite promises to be a success on many levels. That starts with the food." (*San Francisco Chronicle*)

Bienvenue!

Beets Coloriage

2 LBS YELLOW BABY BEETS

2 LBS RED BABY BEETS

2 OZ BALSAMIC VINEGAR
(AGED 20 YEARS)

4 OZ EXTRA VIRGIN OLIVE OIL

1 BUNCH FINE BASIL, JULIENNE

1 OZ BLACK AND WHITE SESAME SEEDS

SALT AND PEPPER TO TASTE

SERVES 6

In a large pot, bring water to a boil. Add the beets. Stir and add salt. Remove when cooked (about 10 to 15 minutes). Peel the beets using a towel or glove. Cut into quarters. Marinate with extra virgin olive oil and basil julienne for about 1 hour. In a sauté pan on medium heat, sizzle the beets. Stir until warm. Remove to a warmed bowl. Drizzle the aged balsamic on top. Sprinkle with sesame seeds. Top with basil julienne. Finish with a turn of the pepper mill.

Lobster Salad

SERVES 6

✤ Combine all ingredients for the Court Bouillon in a large saucepan. Cook to a gentle boil for 30 minutes. Add the lobsters. Stir them around, then cover and cook for 5 minutes. Remove from the pot. Put the lobster on ice water for 5 minutes. Remove it from the water. Clean the meat out of the lobster tail and claw. Divide into 6 portions and set the meat aside.

✤ Combine orange juice, lemon juice and olive oil. Adjust with salt and pepper. Toss the salad with Orange Vinaigrette. Arrange it on 6 plates.

ASSEMBLY

Warm 2 oz butter and 1 tsp crushed garlic in a large sauté pan. Add the lobster meat. Season and place over the salad on the 6 plates. Drizzle with Orange Vinaigrette. Decorate with chervil, tarragon, parsley and a slice of orange. Sprinkle with cayenne pepper.

3 LIVE LOBSTERS, 1 LB EACH
COURT BOUILLON TO COOK THE LOBSTER
1 LB BABY ARUGULA SALAD

✤ COURT BOUILLON
4 CUPS WATER
2 CUPS WHITE WINE
1 CARROT, PEELED AND THINLY SLICED
1 ONION, SLICED
3 CLOVES GARLIC, CRUSHED
1 BAY LEAF

✤ ORANGE VINAIGRETTE
1/2 CUP ORANGE JUICE
1 CUP OLIVE OIL
1/4 CUP LEMON JUICE

1 BUNCH CHERVIL
1 BUNCH TARRAGON
1 BUNCH PARSLEY
SEA SALT
CAYENNE PEPPER
2 OZ BUTTER
1 OZ GARLIC
6 ORANGE SLICES

125

Bouillabaisse Provençale

SERVES 6

Prepare the fish, shellfish and prawns. Separate the fish with firm flesh—scorpion fish, greater weaver fish, angler fish, gurnard—from the ones with light-textured flesh—whiting, sea bass and John Dory.

Gently cook onions in 8 tbsp of olive oil. Do not brown. Add the tomatoes to the onions, followed by the bouquet garni, orange zest, garlic and saffron. Season with salt and pepper.

Lay the firm-fleshed fish, starting with the prawns, on top of the vegetables. Pour the remaining olive oil over the fish. Let sit and infuse for 10 minutes.

17 1/2 LB FRESH MEDITERRANEAN FISH:
SCORPION FISH, GREATER WEAVER FISH,
MONKFISH, GURNARD, WHITING,
BLACK BASS, JOHN DORY,
18 MUSSELS, 18 CLAMS, AND
6 LARGE PRAWNS
2 LARGE ONIONS,
FINELY CHOPPED
12 TBSP OLIVE OIL
4 TOMATOES, PEELED AND DICED
1 BOUQUET GARNI

(continued)

1 STRIP UNTREATED ORANGE ZEST
4 CLOVES GARLIC, CRUSHED
FRESHLY MILLED SALT AND PEPPER
1/2" THICK SLICES RUSTIC BREAD,
LIGHTLY TOASTED IN THE OVEN

✤ ROUILLE
(PIQUANT SAUCE TO
ACCOMPANY FISH SOUP)
2 CLOVES OF GARLIC, PEELED
2 RED CHILIS, CLEANED
CAYENNE PEPPER
PINCH OF SAFFRON
2 TBSP BREADCRUMBS,
SOAKED IN FISH STOCK
2/3 CUP OLIVE OIL

Carefully add enough boiling water to cover the fish. Bring quickly to a boil. Simmer strongly for 5 minutes. Add the light-textured fish and the clams and mussels. Boil vigorously for another 5 to 7 minutes. (A good bouillabaisse needs to boil vigorously for 10 to 15 minutes in order to combine the oil and soup.)

✤ Peel the garlic and pound with the chilis in a mortar. Season with cayenne and saffron. Squeeze out the breadcrumbs and mix with the seasonings. Beat in the oil 1 drop at a time until the sauce has a similar consistency to mustard.

Place a slice of bread on each soup plate and pour in the liquid soup, fish and shellfish. Serve the Rouille separately. If you'd like, potatoes can be cooked with the fish for this soup. They are quartered and layered on top of the vegetables.

Lemon Tart

✤ MEYER LEMON CREAM
1 CUP SUGAR
ZEST OF 4 MEYER LEMONS, REMOVED
WITH A ZESTER AND FINELY CHOPPED
4 LARGE EGGS
3/4 CUP FRESHLY SQUEEZED LEMON
JUICE (FROM 4 TO 5 LEMONS)
2 STICKS PLUS 5 TBSP (10 1/2 OZ)
UNSALTED BUTTER, CUT INTO
TBSP-SIZED PIECES, SOFTENED

SERVES 6

✤ Put a saucepan of water over heat and bring to simmer. Place the sugar and lemon zest in a large metal bowl that can be fitted into the pan of simmering water. Off the heat, rub the sugar and zest together between your fingers until the sugar is moist, grainy and very aromatic. Whisk in the eggs and then the lemon juice.

Fit the bowl into the pan of simmering water making certain that the water doesn't touch the bottom of the bowl. Cook, stirring with the whisk, until the cream thickens and reaches 180° (as measured on an instant-read thermometer).

As you cook the cream, whisking all the while to keep the eggs from overheating and scrambling, you'll see that at first the cream is light and foamy, then the bubbles get larger and finally, as the cream starts to thicken, the whisk leaves tracks. Pay particular attention at this point! The track means the cream is almost ready. Keep whisking. Keep checking the temperature and keep your patience—depending on how much water you've got simmering beneath the bowl, it could take as long as 10 minutes for the cream to reach 180°.

Pull the cream from the heat as soon as it is cooked. Strain it into the container of a blender or food processor or into a clean bowl large enough to beat it with an immersion blender. Let the cream rest at room temperature, stirring occasionally, until it cools to 140°, about 10 minutes.

❧ Place the butter in the bowl of a mixer fitted with the paddle attachment. Beat on low speed until creamy. Add the sugar, almonds, salt, vanilla and eggs. Still working on low speed, beat to blend the ingredients, scraping down the paddle and the sides of the bowls as needed. The dough may look curled—that's all right. With the machine still on low, add the flour in 3 or 4 additions. Mix only until the mixture comes together to form a soft, moist dough—a matter of seconds. Do not overdo it.

❧ To mold the tartlets, butter and set aside six 4 1/2" fluted tartlet tins. Set aside a 5" round biscuit or cookie cutter, preferably fluted (or a cutter that is about 1/2" larger than the diameter of the tartlet tins you're using), 6" square pieces of aluminum foil and some dried pea beans or rice. (You'll use the foil and beans to weight the dough while you bake the shells.)

Working on a floured surface with one piece of dough at a time (keep the other piece in the refrigerator), roll the dough to a thickness of about 1/8". Use the biscuit cutter to cut out as many circles of dough as you can from the rolled-out sheet. Put aside the excess dough for the moment. Fit each round of dough into a buttered tin. To get a good fit without roughing up the dough, use a small ball of excess dough to push the dough into the bottom and up the side of the tin. Place the tins on a jelly-roll pan. Refrigerate them while you roll out, cut and mold the second piece of dough. Place the second set of shells on the jelly-roll pan and chill the tins for 30 minutes. (If you'd like, the dough scraps can be rolled and cut to make additional tartlets. Gather the scraps from both pieces of dough, form them into a disk and cover and chill them for at least an hour before rolling out.)

Center a rack in the oven and preheat to 350°.

Remove the pan with the tartlet tins from the refrigerator. Gently press a square of aluminum foil onto each tin. (The foil should cover the tart shell and extend above the rim). Put a few beans or a spoonful of rice on top of each foil to keep the foil in place. Bake the tartlets for about 15 minutes. Remove the foil and beans and bake the shells for another 2 minutes or so, just until they are lightly colored. Transfer the pan to a rack. Allow the shells to cool to room temperature. (The tartlet shell can be made up to 8 hours ahead and kept at room temperature).

ASSEMBLY

Remove the tartlet shells from their tins. Using a small spoon, fill each shell with the Meyer Lemon Cream. Mound the filling slightly and use the spoon to pat it into a dome. Top each tartlet with a small amount of meringue, a slice of dried lemon chip and a mint leaf. Serve.

❧ SWEET TART DOUGH
2 1/2 STICKS (10 OZ) UNSALTED BUTTER, SOFTENED
1 1/2 CUPS CONFECTIONER'S SUGAR, SIFTED
1/2 CUP (LIGHTLY PACKED) GROUND BLANCHED ALMONDS
1/2 TSP SALT
1/2 TSP VANILLA BEAN PULP OR
1/4 TSP PURE VANILLA EXTRACT
2 LARGE EGGS AT ROOM TEMPERATURE, LIGHTLY BEATEN
3 1/2 CUPS ALL-PURPOSE FLOUR

❧ SHELLS
1/3 RECIPE SWEET TART DOUGH, CUT IN HALF, COVERED AND CHILLED

127

Wine Pairing

LOBSTER SALAD
ESTATE VIOGNIER

BEETS COLORIAGE
ESTATE ROUSSANNE

BOUILLABAISSE PROVENÇALE
GRENACHE

LEMON TART
"ROTTEN LUCK" TBA VIOGNIER

128

Before I was old enough to drink wine (legally), I spent a lot of time wondering why Europe fermented over five hundred different grape varieties while California was using about six. The strangest part was that people only drank two of the six. I was too young to recognize that anyone seriously planning to change how many wine types were being produced in California would have to contend with the American love affair with Cabernet and Chardonnay—our wine equivalents of chocolate and vanilla.

On my twenty-fourth birthday, a friend handed me a glass of Condrieu. Knowing nothing about the wine and informed (erroneously) that it was cheap, I downed what would prove to be one of the most significant gulps of my life. Instantly I could see myself producing the world's greatest six-dollar bottle of wine and hanging out with the Gallo family.

The next day I researched everything UC Davis had on the subject of Condrieu—about twelve sentences. I learned three key facts: Viognier is the grape of Condrieu, it ain't cheap and I'd soon be moving to the Rhône if I wanted to learn more. I immersed myself in everything Rhône. While apprenticing anywhere producers would allow me— from Beaujolais to Provence—I spent a great deal of time organizing climate and soil information. Everything I found indicated that Syrah, Grenache, Viognier and Roussane made sense for California.

It took years to generate commercial quantities of the vines. At a time when there were fewer than fifty acres of Viognier in the world, I propagated thirty-two. Our Roussanne release in 1991 was the second such wine produced globally and the first in the U.S. I am delighted to see Rhône varieties flourish throughout California, and I'm over-whelmed by Robert Parker's declaration in *The Wine Advocate* that I am "the spiritual and qualitative leader of the movement."

As more people have discovered the world beyond chocolate and vanilla, there has been an explosion in plantings in these varieties. Alban Vineyards has provided a large portion of the cuttings needed to see California's Viognier acreage go from zero to over two thousand, and Syrah jump from a few hundred acres to more than seventeen thousand.

ALBAN
VINEYARDS

JOHN ALBAN,
OWNER

8575 ORCUTT ROAD

ARROYO GRANDE, CA 93420

805.546.0305

WWW.ALBANVINEYARDS.COM

TRUFFLED EGGS

SEARED FOIE GRAS WITH CELERY ROOT AND APPLE PURÉE

RIB EYE ROAST WITH ITS OWN HACHIS PARMENTIER

CHOCOLATE ESPRESSO SOUFFLÉ

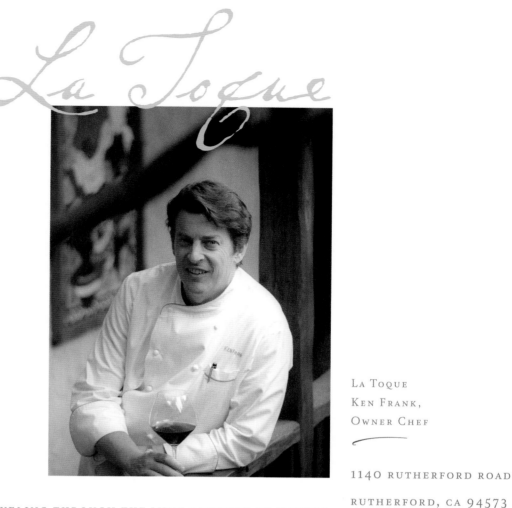

La Toque

La Toque
Ken Frank,
Owner Chef

1140 Rutherford Road

Rutherford, CA 94573

707 963 9770

www.latoque.com

Whether you're traveling through the wine country or making a destination visit specifically for superb dining, La Toque lives up to it's reputation. You smell the vineyards and the grapes long before you pull into La Toque's courtyard. You feel the magic of Napa Valley as you approach the charming adobe hacienda with red tile roof, rough-hewn beams and large stone chimney. Don't let the "hacienda" part fool you. Inside you'll find country French ambience, a gourmand's paradise and a wine lover's dream.

Be prepared to spend an entire evening in this charmingly intimate restaurant adjacent to the Rancho Caymus Inn. Chef Ken Frank serves up a menu of delicate French dishes enlivened with Asian and Mediterranean influences. A first course of Smooth Artichoke Soup with Black Truffle Oil whets your appetite for Roasted Saddle of Lamb with Mustard Spinach Spaetzle or any one of the exquisite selections on the daily menu. In the European style, ripe cheeses with walnut bread are served before you finish with one of La Toque's delicate desserts such as Panna Cotta with just-picked Chandler strawberries. And don't forget the incredible wines. . .

"Half of the fun of being at La Toque is the inspired pairing of the four-glass wine package with the prix fixe five-course tasting menu. The other half is sampling [Chef] Frank's ever-changing array of light, French-inspired dishes."—Martin Booe, *Bon Appétit*

Truffled Eggs

8 FARM FRESH EGGS   SERVES 8

1 FRESH BLACK WINTER TRUFFLE,
WALNUT SIZE   48 hours in advance, carefully place 8 whole fresh eggs and the truffle in

12 TBSP UNSALTED BUTTER   a tightly sealed container. Refrigerate for 2 days, allowing the truffle's

SALT TO TASTE   perfume to permeate the shells and flavor the eggs.

8 SLICES TOASTED BRIOCHE

HOT GLUE GUN AND CLEAR GLUE   Carefully remove the truffled eggs from their jar and stand them back in

EGG TOPPER   a cardboard egg carton. Chop the truffle very fine. Using an egg topper, carefully cut the tops off each egg. Remove the egg. Combine the eggs in a mixing bowl and whisk together with the chopped truffle. Save the empty shells and the little tops.

Put a dot of hot glue in the center of each plate. Immediately attach the empty shell to the plate.

Heat the unsalted butter in a large sauté pan over a low flame. When the butter is melted but not brown, add the egg truffle mixture. Season with 8 good pinches of salt. Cook, stirring constantly with a whisk over low to medium flame until the eggs begin to scramble. (This can easily take 4 or 5 minutes for 8 portions.) Remove from heat and continue stirring until thickened but still very smooth. Ideally, the consistency will be somewhere between scrambled eggs and Hollandaise.

Correct the seasoning. Spoon the mixture into the shells standing on the plates. Place the little shell tops on top and serve with toasted brioche.

Seared Foie Gras with Celery Root and Apple Purée

SERVES 8

1 CELERY ROOT
1 CUP APPLE JUICE
4 OZ UNSALTED BUTTER
2 SIERRA BEAUTY APPLES
(ANY RED APPLE WILL DO)
1 1/4 TO 1 1/2 LBS "GRADE A"
MUSCOVY FOIE GRAS
6 OZ VEAL STOCK
1 1/2 OZ BALSAMIC VINEGAR
SALT AND FRESH GROUND WHITE PEPPER

Peel, dice and cook the celery root with the apple juice, 1 oz of butter and salt until very soft. Purée and reserve warm. Peel and cut the apples into 8 pieces. Sauté in 1 oz butter until tender and golden brown on both sides. Reserve warm.

Reduce veal stock with balsamic vinegar for a few minutes. Whisk in the remaining 2 oz of butter and reserve.

Slice the foie gras into 8 3/8" slices. Generously season with salt and fresh ground white pepper. Sear in a very hot cast iron pan for 20 to 30 seconds on each side.

Place a dollop of the celery root and apple juice purée in the center of each plate. Top with 2 slices of sautéed apple and a slice of foie gras. Spoon the sauce around.

Rib-Eye Roast with Its Own Hachis Permentier

1 6 LB BONELESS RIB-EYE ROAST OF BEEF

2 TBSP VEGETABLE OIL

1 MEDIUM ONION,
CUT INTO 1/2" CHUNKS

1 CARROT, CUT INTO 1/2" CHUNKS

2 STALKS CELERY, CUT
INTO 1/2" CHUNKS

SALT AND FRESHLY GROUND PEPPER

1 BOTTLE (750 ML)
CABERNET SAUVIGNON

4 CUPS VEAL STOCK

6 LARGE YUKON GOLD POTATOES

6 TBSP PLUS ABOUT 2 TBSP
UNSALTED BUTTER

3 OZ FOIE GRAS

1 CLOVE GARLIC, PEELED AND
CUT IN HALF

3 PACKAGES (6 OZ EACH) BABY SPINACH

SERVES 8

Trim the cap or lifter muscle from the roast. Set aside. Tie the remaining eye of beef securely with string at 1 1/2" intervals. Cover and refrigerate. Cut the cap meat into 2" squares. Set aside.

Heat oil in a 10" braising pan over medium heat. Add onion, carrot and celery. Cook, stirring occasionally, until vegetables begin to brown. Season cap meat with salt and pepper to taste. Add to onion mixture. Cook and stir until browned, about 5 more minutes. Spoon off and discard excess fat from pan. Pour in most of the wine, scraping up brown bits from the pan. Add veal stock. Bring mixture to a boil. Reduce heat to low and cook, partially covered, until the meat is very tender and sauce is reduced by about half and has a rich flavor (3 to 4 hours). During cooking, occasionally skim and discard fat and foam from top of mixture.

About 45 minutes before hachis mixture is ready, bake potatoes in a 425° oven until tender when pierced. Let stand until cool enough to handle.

In food processor, combine the 6 tbsp butter and foie gras. Whirl until puréed. Press through a fine strainer into a bowl. Set mixture aside.

Let roast stand at room temperature for about 45 minutes. Season to taste with salt and pepper. Quickly sear in a large sauté pan over high heat. Turn to brown all sides. Transfer pan with roast to a 500° oven and roast for 12 to 14 minutes until a roasting thermometer inserted in the center registers 135°. Remove from oven. Cover loosely with foil and let rest for 15 minutes.

With a slotted spoon, lift the chopped cap meat from the cooking liquid, reserving meat and liquid separately. Chop meat finely. Cut potatoes in half. Scoop potato out of skins. With a fork, mash potatoes in a bowl with chopped meat, half of the foie gras butter and additional butter as needed, and salt and pepper to taste. Keep mixture warm.

Strain the liquid, discarding the remaining solids. Return liquid to pan and, if necessary, boil gently to thicken. Swirl in remaining foie gras butter.

Rub a wide skillet with garlic. Melt about 1 tbsp of the remaining butter in pan over medium-high heat. Stir in spinach and cook just until wilted. Season to taste with salt.

Place roast on a board and cut into 8 slices. On each plate, spoon an oval of the Hachis Parmentier, then a bed of hot spinach in front of it. Top with a slice of beef and spoon sauce around the meat.

134

Chocolate Espresso Soufflé

SERVES 8

7 TBSP FRESHLY BREWED ESPRESSO
10 OZ BITTERSWEET CHOCOLATE
GRANULATED SUGAR FOR RAMEKINS
8 EGG WHITES
2 TBSP POWDERED SUGAR, PLUS MORE
FOR GARNISH
6 EGG YOLKS
WHIPPED CREAM OR ESPRESSO ICE
CREAM (OPTIONAL)
8 4-5 OZ INDIVIDUAL SOUFFLE RAMEKINS

Preheat oven to 400°.

Melt chocolate over a double boiler until warm (about the temperature of a warm bath), not hot.

While the chocolate is melting, thoroughly butter the inside of the ramekins all the way to the top. Thoroughly coat the inside of the ramekins with granulated sugar by pouring in a couple spoonfuls of sugar and then pouring it back out as you rotate the ramekin. This perfectly even coating is the secret to the even rising of your soufflé, so don't touch the inside surface.

Separate the eggs, putting 6 yolks aside to add later. Place the 8 egg whites in a clean dry bowl to make meringue. Whip the whites until frothy. Add 1 tbsp powdered sugar. Continue whipping until they hold a firm smooth peak. Do not beat until hard or the meringue will become more unstable and the soufflé won't rise as well.

Set the meringue aside for a moment. Add the 6 egg yolks to the bowl with the warm chocolate. Whisk them into the chocolate. Add the espresso while continuing to mix quickly until smooth. With a rubber spatula, fold the meringue into the warm chocolate/egg yolk/espresso mixture gently but thoroughly. Do not over mix.

Fill the ramekins to the top and bake in preheated oven for 8 minutes. Sprinkle with powdered sugar. It's best served with a dollop of whipped cream or espresso ice cream on top.

135

Wine Pairing

TRUFFLED EGGS
2003 MINER PINOT NOIR,
GARYS' VINEYARD, SANTA LUCIA HIGHLANDS

SEARED FOIE GRAS WITH CELERY ROOT AND APPLE PURÉE
2004 MINER VIOGNIER,
SIMPSON VINEYARD

RIB EYE ROAST WITH ITS OWN HACHIS PERMENTIER
2002 MINER "THE ORACLE"
NAPA VALLEY RED WINE

CHOCOLATE ESPRESSO SOUFFLÉ
2002 MINER CABERNET SAUVIGNON,
OAKVILLE

136

MINER FAMILY
WINERY

DAVE AND EMILY MINER,
OWNERS

7850 SILVERADO TRAIL

OAKVILLE, CA 94562

707. 944. 9500

WWW.MINERWINES.COM

TUCKED INTO THE EASTERN HILLS OF THE OAKVILLE APPELLATION within the heart of Napa Valley sits Miner Family Vineyards. Founded in 1998 by Dave and Emily Miner along with Dave's folks Ed and Norma, Miner is know for its sensational portfolio of wines. In only a few short years, Miner has identified, sought and secured a number of California's finest vineyard sites to produce and showcase a wide array of varietals.

Miner wines are crafted for the table, not necessarily the critics. Our goal is to construct wines that embrace and enhance the dining experience, and not become it. That said, our white wines are far from meek and mild. Back in 1997, it was our Chardonnay that put us on the radar and we have remained fiercely true to the varietal ever since. These wines are carefully measured for the correct balance of abundant fruit, vibrant acidity and warm oak. Not to be overshadowed, our Viognier has become something of a sensation, particularly to restaurateurs across the country looking for a suitable, chef–friendly alternative to white wine business–as–usual.

Miner Family Vineyards is also known for our powerhouse collection of red wines led by our signature superstar Miner Cabernet Sauvignon, Oakville. We first produced this wine in 1996, a vintage that immediately captured the attention of critics and the hearts of knowing consumers. All of the Miner Family red wines are designed by Mother Nature and challenging vineyard conditions for early consumption and easy maturity.

The combination of excellent vineyard sites along with passionate and thoughtful winemaking injects the necessary components for creating profoundly joyful wines.

On behalf of Miner Family Vineyards, we welcome all of you to join us in our ongoing search for bottled nirvana.

INDIAN SPICED LAMB BURGERS WITH TOASTED CUMIN YOGURT SAUCE AND ONION CHUTNEY

PAN SEARED DAYBOAT SCALLOPS WITH KABOCHA SQUASH PURÉE,
WILTED RAINBOW CHARD AND SAGE BROWN BUTTER

SLOW BRAISED BEEF CHEEKS WITH SPRING ONION MASHED POTATOES
AND SAUTÉED WILD MUSHROOMS

STAR ANISE AND CHILI MOLTEN CAKE WITH CINNAMON–CARAMEL SAUCE

Levende

LEVENDE LOUNGE
KIRI ESCHELLE,
DIRK KAHL AND
BEN DOREN,
OWNERS
JAMIE LAUREN,
CHEF

1710 MISSION STREET

SAN FRANCISCO, CA 94103

415.864.5585

WWW.LEVENDESF.COM

IF YOU'RE LOOKING FOR SOMETHING DIFFERENT, THE HOT NEW ARRIVAL on the San Francisco scene is Levende Lounge. The place to be, Levende provides a sophisticated yet comfortable dining establishment where exceptional cuisine, excellent service, warm ambiance and state-of-the-art sound merge to form a stylish and welcoming entertainment atmosphere.

Levende Lounge boasts elements of high style, both in its architecture and custom décor. Sit back in your plush leather and suede couch where you can enjoy the offerings of a full bar and cocktail menu complemented by eclectic, internationally inspired small plates by *San Francisco Chronicle*'s rising star Chef Jamie Lauren. Food and drinks are elegantly presented and served by a knowledgeable, friendly and fun staff.

Both entertainment and art abound at the Levende, as the Lounge plays host to the finest international and local DJs, live musicians and nightly entertainment. Where else can you savor the food of Mediterranean, Asian and Middle Eastern cultures as you enjoy up-and-coming artists of San Francisco? Enjoy it all at Levende Lounge.

Indian Spiced Lamb Burgers with Toasted Cumin Yogurt Sauce and Onion Chutney

❖ ONION CHUTNEY

2 MEDIUM YELLOW ONIONS, MINCED
1/2 TSP CAYENNE
1/2 TSP TURMERIC
1 TBSP METHI (DRIED LEAF FORM)
2 TBSP LEMON JUICE, TO TASTE
1/4 CUP CANOLA OIL
3 OZ TOMATO PASTE
SALT TO TASTE
SUGAR TO TASTE

❖ CUCUMBERS

2 ENGLISH CUCUMBERS
3 TBSP SALT

❖ BRINE

1 PINT APPLE CIDER VINEGAR
1 PINT SUGAR
10 CLOVES GARLIC
1 TBSP CUMIN SEEDS, TOASTED

❖ MINI LAMB BURGERS

2 1/2 LB LAMB, GROUND
5 CLOVES GARLIC, MINCED
1/4 CUP GINGER, MINCED
1/2 YELLOW ONION, MINCED
1/4 BUNCH EACH CILANTRO, BASIL AND MINT, CHOPPED
1/2 TBSP GROUND CORIANDER
1/2 TSP TURMERIC
1/4 TSP CAYENNE
1/4 TSP GROUND NUTMEG
1/4 TSP GROUND CLOVES
1/2 TBSP SALT
1/4 TSP GROUND BLACK PEPPER

❖ YOGURT SAUCE

1 QT THICK PLAIN YOGURT
1 1/2 TBSP MINT, CHOPPED
1 TSP SALT
2 CLOVES GARLIC, MINCED
1/2 LEMON, ZESTED
1 TBSP CUMIN SEEDS
1/4 TSP BLACK PEPPER

SERVES 10

❖ Combine all ingredients. Add salt and sugar to taste. Let sit for at least 1 hour before serving. (It is better if it sits overnight.) Serve at room temperature. To garnish burgers, place about 1 tsp of chutney on each burger.

❖ Slice cucumbers thin (double paper thickness) on a mandolin. Place sliced cucumbers in a single layer on a perforated surface. Make sure to put another pan underneath to catch juices that will ultimately leach out. Sprinkle with salt in an even layer making sure all cucumbers get a little salt. Let it macerate at room temperature about 1 hour.

❖ In a saucepan, combine all ingredients. Bring to a boil. Take off heat and let cool.

Squeeze cucumbers in small bundles until most of their juice comes out. Place cucumbers in a plastic container with a lid. Pour chilled brine over cucumbers. Cover and let sit refrigerated at least 24 hours. During this time, shake the pickles once or twice. These will last for weeks.

❖ Combine all ingredients and form into 1 1/2 oz patties.

❖ Toast cumin seeds over medium heat until aromatic. Grind in a spice grinder. Combine with all other ingredients and check seasoning.

ASSEMBLY

Season burgers with salt. Grill until medium to allow all the flavors to develop. Serve on mini buns and top with onion chutney and yogurt sauce. Serve pickles on the side.

Pan Seared Dayboat Scallops with Kabocha Squash Purée, Wilted Rainbow Chard and Sage Brown Butter

SERVES 4

❧ Preheat oven to 375°. Line a baking sheet with parchment paper. Season with olive oil. Cut squash in half lengthwise. Place flesh side down on greased parchment paper. Roast in oven about 45 minutes or until soft. Heat cream and butter until hot. Scoop seeds out of the squash and discard the skin, saving only the flesh. Working in 2 stages, process the squash in a food processor. Add half the cream mixture and half the cinnamon to each batch until a smooth purée forms. Season with salt. Reserve warm.

❧ In a small saucepan, heat butter and sage stems until butter is melted. Simmer over low heat until butter solids caramelize and begin to smell nutty. The color should resemble caramel. Strain through a fine strainer and keep warm.

❧ Clean chard by cutting center rib out of each leaf. Cut the leafs into 1" squares and rinse with water. In a sauté pan, heat 1 tbsp olive oil with the garlic and sauté until the garlic becomes aromatic. Season with a touch of salt. Add chard and sauté briefly. Season with salt. Add about 4 oz of water (or stock). Continue to sauté until chard is soft but still retains a slight crunch. Check seasoning.

❧ Heat a sauté pan (non-stick is okay, but not preferred) over high heat until smoking. Season the scallops with salt on both sides. Place about 2 tbsp canola oil in sauté pan and let it smoke a little. Add the scallops and turn heat down to medium. Cook about 3 minutes until the scallops turn golden brown. Flip the scallops and turn the heat off the pan. Add 1 tbsp butter and allow to melt. Using a spoon, baste the scallops with the melted butter in the pan. Set aside.

ASSEMBLY

Spoon a small mound of squash purée in the center of each plate. Top with some of the sautéed chard. Place 3 scallops on the edge of the chard. Spoon 1/2 tbsp brown butter on each of the scallops. Garnish with sliced sage and ground nutmeg.

❧ SQUASH PURÉE
2 MEDIUM SIZE KABOCHA SQUASH
OLIVE OIL
1/4 CUP HEAVY CREAM
4 TBSP BUTTER
1/2 TSP GROUND CINNAMON
SALT TO TASTE

❧ SAGE BROWN BUTTER
1 LB BUTTER
1 BUNCH SAGE, STEMS ONLY, CHOPPED

❧ CHARD
3 BUNCHES RAINBOW CHARD
8 CLOVES GARLIC, MINCED
OLIVE OIL
SALT TO TASTE
WATER (OR VEGETABLE STOCK)

❧ SCALLOPS
12 LARGE SCALLOPS
CANOLA OIL
SALT TO TASTE
4 SAGE LEAVES, PICKED
1 TSP GROUND NUTMEG

141

Slow Braised Beef Cheeks with Spring Onion Mashed Potatoes and Sautéed Wild Mushrooms

❖ CHEEKS

SERVES 4

5 LB BEEF CHEEKS

WONDRA FLOUR FOR DUSTING

6 CARROTS, CUT INTO 1" PIECES

2 YELLOW ONIONS, CUT IN QUARTERS

1/4 BUNCH CELERY, CUT INTO 1" PIECES

1/2 BUNCH THYME

1/2 BUNCH ROSEMARY

2 CUPS DRY RED WINE

2 TBSP BLACK PEPPERCORNS

1 HEAD GARLIC, CUT IN HALF

CHICKEN STOCK TO COVER

(ABOUT 1 GALLON)

8 TBSP CANOLA OIL

CHIVES, CHOPPED

SALT TO TASTE

❖ Preheat oven to 350°. Clean excess fat and membranes off the beef cheeks. Season with salt and sprinkle with Wondra flour. Heat a non-stick sauté pan until smoking. Add 4 tbsp canola oil and let smoke. Place beef cheeks in the sauté pan and sear until darkly caramelized. Set cheeks aside to rest.

Heat a large braising pan on top of the stove until smoking. Add 4 tbsp canola oil and heat until smoking. Add all the vegetables, herbs and peppercorns and cook until soft. Deglaze with red wine and reduce by half. Add the beef cheeks to the braising pan and cover with chicken stock. Bring to a simmer on top of the stove. Cover the direct surface of the liquid with a piece of parchment paper and a piece of tinfoil. Place another piece of tinfoil on the entire pan to create both a cover as well as a tight seal.

❖ MASHED POTATOES

4 RUSSET POTATOES, PEELED

AND QUARTERED

6 CLOVES GARLIC

6 TBSP BUTTER

1 CUP HEAVY CREAM

6 SPRING ONIONS, DICED

SALT TO TASTE

Place in the oven and braise slowly (small bubbles should be constant throughout the process). Cook for 3 to 5 hours. The beef cheeks are done when they are tender to the touch but still firm enough to stay together. Cool overnight in liquid.

The following day, remove the cheeks from the pan and wipe off gelatinous stock. Set aside. Place the cooking liquid (with the veggies) in a saucepan and reduce until sauce consistency. Strain and hold.

❖ MUSHROOMS

2 LB WILD MUSHROOMS, CLEANED

(WHATEVER TYPE IS IN SEASON)

6 CLOVES GARLIC, MINCED

4 TBSP THYME, CHOPPED

1/4 CUP RED WINE

CANOLA OIL

2 TBSP BUTTER

SALT TO TASTE

❖ Place the potatoes and garlic in a saucepan and cover with cold water. Add 1 tbsp salt and bring to a simmer. Cook until potatoes are soft. Sauté the diced spring onions in 2 tbsp of the butter. Add 1/2 cup of the heavy cream. Season with salt and reduce until thick. Set aside. Heat the remaining butter and cream until hot. Strain the potatoes. Using a ricer or stand mixer, mix together the hot potatoes, the hot cream mixture and the spring onion mixture. Check seasoning and keep warm.

❖ Heat 2 sauté pans until smoking. Add 1 tbsp of canola oil to each. Wait until the oil gets hot. Add half the mushrooms to each pan. Sauté briefly to get some color on the mushrooms. Add 1 tbsp butter to each pan, half the thyme and half the garlic. Season with salt. Cook about 30 seconds until the garlic gets toasty. Add red wine and reduce by half. Keep warm.

142

ASSEMBLY

Preheat oven to 400°. Cut the beef cheeks into 2 pieces. Place in a sauté pan and cover with some of the cooking liquid. Place in the oven and cook until the liquid has reduced slightly and the cheeks are hot. Spoon a small pile of mashed potatoes on each plate and place some of the mushrooms in the center. When the cheeks are hot, add 1/2 tbsp of butter in the pan. Swirl it in to give the sauce a nice sheen. Place the cheeks on top of the potatoes. Spoon sauce over them. Top with chopped chives.

Star Anise and Chili Molten Cake with Cinnamon-Caramel Sauce

SERVES 8

❧ CAKE

12 WHOLE EGGS
12 EGG YOLKS
21 OZ BITTERSWEET CHOCOLATE
1 1/4 LB UNSALTED BUTTER
1 CUP SIFTED FLOUR
3 CUPS SUGAR
1/2 TSP SALT
6 PIECES STAR ANISE
2 TBSP DRIED KOREAN RED CHILI
2 CINNAMON STICKS
16-20 4 OZ COOKING MOLDS

143

❧ Preheat oven to 325°. Combine the spices in a sauté pan and cook until aromatic and toasted. Grind the spices in a spice grinder. Set aside. Combine chocolate and butter in a heatproof bowl. Place over water of a double boiler. Heat until smooth and melted. Turn off the heat, add the spices and sugar to the chocolate–butter mixture and let cool.

Combine eggs, egg yolks and salt. Whisk until smooth. Set aside. Grease 4 oz cooking molds with cooking spray or butter. Fold approximately 2 cups of the chocolate mixture into the eggs. Add the rest. Using a whisk, stir in the flour just to combine. Pour batter into greased molds. Cook 10 to 12 minutes if using a convection oven, a little longer if using a still oven. The cake should be set on the outside but still gooey in the center. Let cool. Serve or save for later and reheat.

❧ CARAMEL SAUCE

1 CUP SUGAR
WATER TO COVER
4 TBSP UNSALTED BUTTER
1/2 CUP HEAVY CREAM
1 TSP GROUND CINNAMON
PINCH OF SALT

❧ In a saucepan, add the sugar and cover with cold water. (The water should just cover the surface of the sugar.) Heat until the sugar begins to caramelize and the water evaporates, about 10 minutes. Whisk in the butter and stir until it is incorporated. Add the cream, salt and cinnamon. It will take on a sauce consistency. When cool, taste for seasoning.

ASSEMBLY

Heat the molten cake until warm throughout. Serve with a drizzle of the caramel sauce and a dollop of whipped cream. Finish with a sprinkling of cinnamon sugar.

Wine Pairing

Indian Spiced Lamb Burgers
2002 Le Cigare Volant

Celery Root and Fennel Soup
2004 Il Circo Erbaluce "La Funambola"

Pan Seared Scallops with Brown Sage Butter
2004 Pacific Rim Riesling

Star Anise and Chili Molten Cake
with Cinnamon–Caramel Sauce
Framboise, Infusion of Raspberries

144

RANDALL GRAHM WAS BORN IN Los Angeles in 1953 and attended Uncle Charlie's Summer Camp, excuse me, the prestigious University of California at Santa Cruz where he was a permanent Liberal Arts major. Some time later he found himself sweeping floors at the Wine Merchant in Beverly Hills. Through exceptional fortune he was given the opportunity to taste a good number of great French wines and this singular experience turned him into a complete and insufferable wine fanatic. He returned to the University of California at Davis to complete a degree in viticulture in 1979, where he developed a single-minded obsession with Pinot Noir.

After attempts to produce the Great American Pinot Noir proved systematically elusive, he turned his attention to the Rhône varieties. His vineyard was planted to Syrah, Roussanne, Marsanne and Viognier and produced achingly beautiful wines. As symptomatic of his chronic wanderlust, in the late 1980s Mr. Grahm felt compelled to cast his net further afield and thus began the great Italianate plantings in Bonny Doon's Ca' del Solo vineyard. This Monterey County property has been or soon may be planted to an ever-expanding roster of Italianate varieties such as Nebbiolo, Barbera, Pinot Grigio, Dolcetto, Freisa, Aglianico, Teroldego, Ciliegiolo and Sagrantino.

Bonny Doon Vineyard produces a wide variety of estimable products, most notably Le Cigare Volant, Muscat Vin de Glacière, Big House Red and Cardinal Zin. We collaborate on several wines produced in Italy which we sell under the protective aegis of the brand "Il Circo," and we import two wines from France—Domaine des Blagueurs Syrah-Sirrah and Madiran Heart of Darkness.

There are certain precepts we believe in at Bonny Doon—have as much fun with the enterprise of winemaking as the relevant governmental agencies will allow; produce wine and wine labels that will scintillate the most jaded imbiber; pay particularly close attention to the old chestnut that wine is produced in the vineyard; walk the walk by employing biodynamic viticultural practices in our own properties and encourage our grape suppliers to do the same; and retain as much of the natural qualities of the grapes through minimal cellar treatment. This includes eschewing limpidity for its own sake and relying on gravity to render matters perfectly clear.

You can sample the eclectic products of Bonny Doon in restaurants and retail shops, as well as our tasting rooms in Santa Cruz and Paso Robles.

BONNY DOON
VINEYARD

RANDALL GRAHM,
OWNER

PO BOX 8376

SANTA CRUZ, CA 95061

831.425.3625

WWW.BONNYDOONVINEYARD.COM

GOAT CHEESE FONDUE

WATERCRESS SALAD WITH BLEU CHEESE DRESSING

"COUS COUS 404" WITH GRILLED LAMB SKEWERS AND SPICY CHICK PEA STEW

LUNA S'MORES

Luna Park

Luna Park
A.J. Gilbert,
Owner

694 Valencia Street
San Francisco, ca 94110
415.553.8584
www.lunaparksf.com

Where can you find fun, comfort and style at a reasonable price? For great food and a happening place whether you live in San Francisco or are visiting, Luna Park's the place to be. One of three restaurants owned by A.J. Gilbert (the other two are Kitchen & Cocktails in Manhattan and Luna Park Los Angeles), Luna Park is located on Valencia Street, the up-and-coming restaurant and bar scene in the Mission District. Luna Park's décor includes dark red walls, subdued lighting and an eclectic mix of amusement park regalia, crazy artwork and a hopping bar scene. Relax with your friends in your booth or with new friends at your bar stool, grab a "Kick @#** Mai Tai" or a "You're a Pepper Too" and dig in! Tonight's the night to enjoy good eating without paying a king's ransom.

The menu, mostly French and Italian with a few American and Asian accents, is simple without sacrificing excitement. Begin with Warm Goat Cheese Fondue or Marinated Hawaiian Tuna "Poke" with Fried Wonton Chips and work your way through the delicious Fontina Stuffed Ravioli with Mushrooms, Spinach and Truffle Oil or Breaded Pork Cutlet Stuffed with Mushrooms and Gruyere Cheese with Mashed Potatoes, String Beans and Apple-Cranberry Sauce. Don't forget to take a trip down nostalgia lane with Make Your Own S'mores just like your camp leader used to make.

Goat Cheese Fondue

2 CUPS HEAVY CREAM
2 LBS FRENCH COUTURIER GOAT CHEESE
OR OTHER FRESH CHEVRE GOAT CHEESE,
CRUMBLED
2 GRANNY SMITH APPLES,
CORED AND SLICED
1/2 FRESH BAGUETTE, SLICED
SALT AND PEPPER TO TASTE

SERVES 4

Heat a medium size ceramic serving dish in the oven until warm. In a heavy saucepan over medium heat, cook the cream until it is reduced by 1/2. Add crumbled goat cheese to the hot cream. Whisk until smooth. Serve in the heated serving dish with bread and sliced apples as accompaniments.

148

Watercress Salad with Bleu Cheese Dressing

1 1/2 SHALLOTS, MINCED
10 OZ BLUE CHEESE
1/3 CUP SHERRY VINEGAR
1 TBSP SALT
1 TSP BLACK PEPPER
1 1/2 CUPS REGULAR OLIVE OIL
2/3 CUP EXTRA VIRGIN OLIVE OIL
10 OZ FRESH WATERCRESS,
RINSED AND DRIED
1 OZ HAZELNUTS, TOASTED
6 OZ CAMBOZOLA CHEESE, CRUMBLED
1 BARTLETT PEAR, CORED
AND THINLY SLICED

SERVES 4

Make the dressing by combing all ingredients except for the oil in the bowl of a mixer. With the mixer running, add the oils very slowly, beating until the dressing emulsifies. Set aside.

Place the watercress in a large bowl. Add 1/2 cup of the salad dressing. Toss the watercress until well coated with the dressing. Arrange the watercress on 4 plates. Arrange the hazelnuts, cambozola and sliced pear on each plate in a decorative manner. Serve immediately.

"Cous Cous 404" with Grilled Lamb Skewers and Spicy Chick Pea Stew

SERVES 4

✤ Place the olive oil in a large saucepan over low heat. Add the onions to the pan. Cook until translucent but do not brown. Add the garbanzo beans and wine to the pan. Increase the heat to medium. Continue to cook until the wine has evaporated. Stir in the pomi tomatoes, chili powder and salt. Add the vegetable stock and the carrots. Simmer until the carrots are tender, adding stock only if necessary. The finished stew should have only enough liquid to stay moist.

✤ In a large saucepan over medium heat, cook the garlic and onions in olive oil until translucent, stirring occasionally with a wooden spoon. Add the saffron to the pan. Stir until the saffron is well distributed. Add the wine to the pan. Continue cooking until all the wine has evaporated. Stir in the Pomi tomatoes, tomato paste, fennel, coriander and harissa. Add the vegetable stock to the pan and bring to a boil. Reduce the heat to low. Let simmer for 20 minutes. Add salt to taste. Set aside.

✤ Combine the couscous, salt and saffron in a medium size bowl. Pour the boiling water over the couscous, stirring well. Cover the bowl tightly. Let sit for 15 minutes or until all the liquid is absorbed.

✤ CHICK PEA STEW

1 CUP WHITE OR YELLOW ONION, FINELY DICED

2 TBSP OLIVE OIL

2 CANS GARBANZO BEANS, DRAINED

1/4 CUP WHITE WINE

6 1/2 OZ POMI TOMATOES OR OTHER CRUSHED TOMATOES

1 1/2 TSP CAYENNE PEPPER

2 1/2 TBSP CHILI POWDER

5 CUPS VEGETABLE STOCK OR TO TASTE

2 CUPS CARROT, PEELED AND CUT INTO 1/2" DICE

1 TSP SALT PLUS ADDITIONAL TO TASTE

✤ LAMB SAFFRON SAUCE

1 TBSP GARLIC

1 CUP WHITE OR YELLOW ONION, CUT INTO 1/2" DICE

2 TBSP OLIVE OIL

2 PINCHES SAFFRON

2 TBSP WHITE WINE

13 OZ POMI TOMATOES OR OTHER CRUSHED TOMATOES

2 TBSP TOMATO PASTE

1 TBSP FENNEL SEED, TOASTED AND GROUND

1 TBSP CORIANDER, TOASTED AND GROUND

2 1/2 TBSP HARISSA

8 CUPS VEGETABLE STOCK

SALT TO TASTE

✤ COUSCOUS

1 CUP COUSCOUS

1 TSP SALT

1 PINCH SAFFRON

1 CUP BOILING WATER

(continued)

149

❖ LAMB SKEWERS

1/4 CUP SALT
1 TSP GROUND FENNEL SEED
1 TSP GROUND CORIANDER
1/2 TSP GROUND CUMIN
2 TSP MINCED ROSEMARY
1 TSP GROUND CHILE DE ARBOL
1 PINCH GROUND BLACK PEPPER
16 OZ LAMB SIRLOIN,
CUT INTO 1 OZ PIECES
2 RED BELL PEPPERS,
CUT INTO 2" SQUARES
1 MEDIUM SIZE CHINESE EGGPLANT,
CUT INTO 1/2" SLICES
4 LINKS LAMB SAUSAGE, EACH
CUT IN HALF
1 RED ONION,
CUT INTO 1 1/2" SQUARES
8 CRIMINI MUSHROOMS
8 METAL OR BAMBOO SKEWERS

❖ Preheat a broiler or grill. In a small bowl, stir together the salt with the fennel seed, coriander, cumin, rosemary, chile de arbol and black pepper. Sprinkle the mixture over the pieces of lamb sirloin. Alternate the lamb, bell pepper, eggplant, lamb sausage, red onion and crimini mushrooms on 8 metal or bamboo skewers. Broil or grill the skewers until they reach desired doneness, turning them to prevent burning, about 15 to 20 minutes. Set aside.

ASSEMBLY

Divide the couscous between 4 serving dishes or bowls. Ladle 1/2 cup of the garbanzo bean stew over the couscous. Arrange 2 skewers on top. Add sauce to moisten. Serve immediately.

Luna S'mores

❖ GRAHAM CRACKERS

1/2 CUP GRANULATED SUGAR
1 CUP BROWN SUGAR
1 CUP PASTRY FLOUR
2 CUPS GRAHAM FLOUR PLUS
ADDITIONAL FOR DUSTING
1/2 TSP BAKING POWDER
PINCH OF SALT
1/2 CUP SHORTENING
1/2 TSP VANILLA EXTRACT
1/2 CUP WHOLE MILK

SERVES 4

❖ Preheat oven to 375°.

Place the sugars, flours, baking powder and salt together in the bowl of an electric mixer fitted with a paddle attachment. With the mixer on the lowest setting, stir the dry ingredients together. Add the shortening to the mixing bowl and continue to stir the ingredients together until the mixture resembles coarse sand.

In a small bowl, stir together the vanilla and milk. Add the milk to the flour mixture with the mixer running at slow speed just until it forms a dough. Do not over mix.

Place 1/2 cup of the dough on a lightly floured sheet of parchment paper. Sprinkle lightly with additional flour. Add another sheet of parchment paper. With a rolling pin, roll the dough to a thickness of 1/16". Peel off the top sheet of parchment paper and place the bottom sheet and the dough on a baking sheet. Repeat the process until all the dough has been used.

Bake the dough for 4 minutes. Pull them out and score them with a pizza cutter to form rectangular cracker shapes. Continue baking for 4 to 6 minutes or until golden brown. Cool completely, then break them apart into crackers along the scored lines. Store in an airtight container.

✤ In a small bowl, stir together the cocoa, brown sugar and granulated sugar. Set aside. In a heavy bottom saucepan, bring the cream, butter and salt to a boil over medium heat. Whisk in the cocoa–sugar mixture until it is well combined. Continue to cook until the sauce thickens slightly. Pour the hot fudge into 4 ramekins and keep warm while you broil the marshmallows.

ASSEMBLY

When ready to serve, preheat the oven broiler. Fill 4 ovenproof ramekins with miniature marshmallows. Place the ramekins on a baking sheet and place underneath the broiler at least 5" away from the flame. Broil until the marshmallows bubble up and brown. Each serving gets 1 ramekin of marshmallow, 1 ramekin of hot fudge and 3 to 4 graham crackers.

✤ HOT FUDGE
5 OZ UNSWEETENED COCOA
6 OZ BROWN SUGAR
6 OZ GRANULATED SUGAR
1 1/4 CUPS HEAVY CREAM
8 OZ UNSALTED BUTTER,
CUT INTO SMALL PIECES
1 10 1/2 OZ BAG MINIATURE
MARSHMALLOWS
PINCH OF SALT

Wine Pairing

Goat Cheese Fondue
2002 Syrah

Watercress Salad with Bleu Cheese Dressing
2003 Grenache

"Cous Cous 404" with Grilled Lamb Skewers
and Spicy Chick Pea Stew
2002 Benchland Reserve Syrah

Luna S'mores
2002 Zinfandel

UNTI

DRY CREEK VALLEY

GRENACHE

2 0 0 3

82% GRENACHE · 11% SYRAH · 7% MOURVEDRE

GROWN, PRODUCED AND BOTTLED BY UNTI VINEYARDS

HEALDSBURG, CALIFORNIA ALCOHOL 14.9% BY VOLUME

UNTI

VINEYARDS

MICK UNTI,
OWNER

4202 DRY CREEK ROAD

HEALDSBURG, CA 95448

707.433.5540

WWW.UNTIVINEYARDS.COM

"UNTI IS ANOTHER NEW WINERY WORTH REMEMBERING. Winemaker Mick Unti draws grapes from his family's vineyards in the middle of the Zinfandel-loving Dry Creek Valley. . . .The wine mixes ripe blackberry notes with suggestions of black pepper and cocoa in it is supple first impression while being reasonably full in body. It will age comfortably for several years." *Los Angeles Times*

"Unti is the type of winery that exemplifies the unpretentious, down-to-earth approach to winemaking that we associate with great Sonoma County producers. Unti's wines are never fancy or over-done, though styled for those of us who love robust California wines to drink, not just to hoard or collect. . . .Unti's 1999 Dry Creek Valley Zinfandel is blended with a tiny bit of Syrah and Petite Sirah for color and structure. The wine is full of briary, brambly berry fruit with a memorable mid-palate and finish. It is the type of Zinfandel that makes you feel happy. We first tasted the 1999 Dry Creek Valley Syrah after only five months in bottle and even then it showed a wonderfully meaty, gamy rich quality backed by lots of fruit. Mick Unti calls the wine 'brothy' and if you've ever tasted consommé that has been made over a long time, you'll recognize that depth of flavor. Many of San Francisco's hippest and tastiest restaurants are pouring this wine by the glass, so if you've been wondering where to get your hands on this Syrah, here it is!" *The Wine House*

Braised Wild Burgundy Escargots with Navy Beans, Garlic, Pernod and Fennel Salad

Warm Sweetbread Salad with Bacon, Sherry Vinegar, Shiitakes and Whole Grain Mustard

Roasted Poussin with Gigante Beans, Haricot Verts and Roasted Red Bell Peppers

Rocher aux Amandes

MYTH
SEAN O'BRIEN,
EXECUTIVE CHEF
AND PARTNER

470 PACIFIC STREET
SAN FRANCISCO, CA 94133
415.677.8986
WWW.MYTHSF.COM

MYTH IS TUCKED INTO A QUIET CORNER OF SAN FRANCISCO'S HISTORIC antique and design district known as Jackson Square. Within walking distance of the Financial District, North Beach and Chinatown, Myth turns dining into an epicurean experience by bringing a blast of fresh air and casual elegance to the table. The ambience lends a casual, warm but loungy feel with rich walnut carriage booths, Japanese inspired lamps and a view of the bar through imported glass. A tinge of minimalism and a slight hint of industrialism combine to create an environment filled with warmth and intriguing intellectuality.

With banquettes covered in lush Japanese style prints, there isn't a bad seat in the house. The restaurant boasts several sexy private dining spaces—cozy tables for romantic evenings—as well as the central dining area for the more action-oriented crowd.

Chef Sean O'Brien puts his years of training at Gary Danko to good use as he creates what Myth's interior presents to your senses, an experience you'll want to savor. Begin your evening with Ahi Tuna Poke with Cucumber, Shiso, Limu, Tatsoi and Kukui Nut. Or enjoy his Garganelli Pasta with Foie Gras Cream, Maitake Mushrooms and Marsala. Each meal is served in full and half portion sizes to accommodate every appetite.

Myth weaves its own magic with the seductive surroundings, enticing food and value-oriented prices. With all it has to offer, it's no wonder Myth was selected as one of the elite Top 100 Bay Area Restaurants for 2005!

Braised Wild Burgundy Escargot with Navy Beans, Garlic, Pernod and Fennel Salad

❖ ESCARGOT

1 CAN OF SNAILS (72 COUNT)
1/2 CUP FENNEL, MINCED
3 TBSP GARLIC, MINCED
3 TBSP SHALLOTS, MINCED
3 TBSP EXTRA VIRGIN OLIVE OIL
3 TBSP UNSALTED BUTTER
3 TBSP PARSLEY, MINCED
1 TBSP THYME, MINCED
1/2 TSP ROSEMARY, MINCED
1 TBSP SHERRY WINE
1 TBSP PERNOD

❖ NAVY BEANS

1 CUP NAVY BEANS
1 CARROT, PEELED
1 ONION, PEELED AND QUARTERED
3 SPRIGS FRESH THYME
2 BAY LEAVES, DRIED
4 CUPS CHICKEN STOCK
6 TBSP UNSALTED BUTTER
1 LEMON, JUICED
1 FENNEL BULB, SHAVED THINLY
3 BUNCHES MACHE
KOSHER SALT TO TASTE

SERVES 6

❖ In a sauté pan, heat oil and butter. Over low heat, cook fennel, garlic and shallots until tender. Add snails with the juice from the can and simmer for about 1 hour or until most of the liquid has cooked out. Add sherry wine, Pernod and herbs. Stir to combine.

❖ Soak the navy beans in water overnight. The next day, strain and rinse with fresh water. Cover beans with about 4 cups of chicken stock, carrot, onion, thyme and bay leaves. Bring to a boil. Simmer slowly until tender; about 1 hour. Season with Kosher salt. Add bean mixture to braised escargot. Add the butter. Heat together until butter is emulsified with the chicken stock to form a loose sauce. Correct the rich flavors with the juice of the lemon. Transfer the escargot and beans to bowls. Top with shaved raw fennel.

Warm Sweetbread Salad with Bacon, Sherry Vinegar, Shiitakes and Whole Grain Mustard

SERVES 6

❖ Heat olive oil in a sauté pan and add bacon. Cook until bacon fat is rendered, but not crisp. Remove bacon and add shallots and garlic. Sauté for about 2 minutes. Add sherry vinegar and chicken stock. Simmer until slightly thick, about 5 minutes. Add mustard and soy sauce. Cook for about 1 minute. Add butter and bacon and stir to combine. Keep warm.

❖ Heat clarified butter and add garlic and shallots. Sauté until tender over low heat. Add shiitakes and sauté until tender, about 5 minutes. Add parsley and salt to taste.

❖ Slowly bring sweetbreads up to a simmer with the lemon juice. Simmer about 5 minutes until slightly firm, depending on the size of the sweetbreads. Remove sweatbreads and shock in ice water. Once cooled, clean membranes from sweetbreads. Tear into bite size pieces. Coat with rice flour. Sauté in clarified butter until golden brown and crisp. Remove sweetbreads and wipe out and discard excess butter. Season sweetbreads with Kosher salt.

ASSEMBLY

Toss mushrooms in the pan to reheat along with 6 oz of the vinaigrette, blanched green beans, yellow frisée, mache and sweetbreads. Divide salad mixture and pack into a ring mold, if desired. Garnish plate with excess vinaigrette and minced chives.

❖ VINAIGRETTE

5 TBSP EXTRA VIRGIN OLIVE OIL
5 TBSP SHERRY VINEGAR
1/4 LB SMOKED BACON, MINCED
1 SHALLOT, MINCED
1 GARLIC CLOVE, MINCED
1/2 CUP CHICKEN STOCK
1 TBSP WHOLE GRAIN MUSTARD
1/4 CUP SOY SAUCE
1 TBSP UNSALTED BUTTER

157

❖ SHIITAKE MUSHROOMS

1/4 CUP CLARIFIED BUTTER
1/4 CUP SHALLOTS, MINCED
1 GARLIC CLOVE, MINCED
6 OZ SHIITAKES, STEMS REMOVED
AND QUARTERED
2 TBSP PARSLEY, MINCED
KOSHER SALT TO TASTE

❖ SWEETBREADS

1 LB SWEETBREADS
1/4 CUP RICE FLOUR
1 LEMON, JUICED
KOSHER SALT TO TASTE
3/4 CUP CLARIFIED BUTTER

❖ GARNISH

6 OZ HARICOT VERT, CUT AND
BLANCHED FOR GARNISH
2 HEADS YELLOW FRISEE, CHOPPED
1 CUP SPINACH CHIFFONADE
1 BUNCH CHIVES, MINCED

Roasted Poussin with Gigante Beans, Haricot Verts and Roasted Red Bell Peppers

6 POUSSINS, REMOVE EXCESS FAT, NECK
BONES AND WING TIPS

SERVES 6

❖ MARINADE
2 CUPS WHITE WINE
2 CUPS EXTRA VIRGIN OLIVE OIL
1/2 CUP GARLIC, MINCED
6 TBSP DIJON MUSTARD
2 1/2 TBSP KOSHER SALT
2 TBSP FRESH THYME, MINCED
1 TBSP FRESH ROSEMARY, MINCED
1 TBSP GROUND CORIANDER SEED
1 TBSP GROUND CUMIN SEED
CLARIFIED BUTTER FOR SAUTÉ

❖ GIGANTE BEANS
2 CUPS OF GIGANTE BEANS
8 CUPS OF CHICKEN STOCK,

1/4 LB HARICOT VERTS, CUT INTO 1"
PIECES AND BLANCHED UNTIL
TENDER, ABOUT 5 MINUTES
1 RED BELL PEPPER, ROASTED, PEELED,
SEEDED AND CHOPPED
1 TBSP PARSLEY, MINCED
6 TBSP OF UNSALTED BUTTER
KOSHER SALT
CHIVE BATONS FOR GARNISH

❖ Add all marinade ingredients to a blender, except the oil. Turn on blender and gradually pour in the olive oil to emulsify.

Rub poussins with some of the marinade. Save excess marinade for another use. Refrigerate poussins overnight. The next day, wipe off excess marinade to prevent burning and preheat oven to 500°. In a sauté pan, heat clarified butter over high heat. Carefully place poussins in pan, breast side down. Sear all sides until golden brown. Remove excess fat from pan and place poussins in the oven for about 30 minutes, until cooked through and juices run clear. Season with Kosher salt.

❖ The night before, soak 2 cups of gigante beans in water. The next day, strain and rinse the beans with fresh water. Cover with about 8 cups of chicken stock, bring to a boil and simmer until tender, about 4 hours.

ASSEMBLY

Add cooked haricot verts and roasted and chopped red bell pepper to the gigante beans. Add 6 tbsp of unsalted butter and 1 tbsp of minced parsley. Season with Kosher salt. Place poussin on the bean mixture. Top with a garnish of chive batons.

Rocher aux Amandes

SERVES 6

Preheat oven to 325°.

Make a Swiss meringue by whisking together the egg whites and the powdered sugar in a double boiler over low simmering water until meringue registers 130° on a thermometer. Remove from heat and continue whisking until mixture cools. Using a rubber spatula, fold in the chopped almonds, vanilla and Framboise.

Drop tablespoons of meringue onto a non-stick baking sheet and bake for 12 minutes. Turn off the oven and leave them in for an extra 5 minutes.

Cool rocher on racks before serving. Serve with berries and Crème Fraiche.

3 EGG WHITES
6 OZ POWDERED SUGAR
6 OZ ALMONDS, TOASTED AND CHOPPED
2 TBSP FRAMBOISE LIQUEUR
1 TSP VANILLA EXTRACT

FRESH BERRIES
(YOUR FAVORITE)
CRÈME FRAICHE,
LIGHTLY SWEETENED

Wine Pairing

Braised Wild Burgundy Escargots
with Navy Beans, Garlic, Pernod and Fennel Salad
Peter Michael 2003 L'Après–Midi Estate Sauvignon Blanc

Warm Sweetbread Salad with Bacon, Sherry Vinegar,
Shiitakes and Whole Grain Mustard
Peter Michael 2003 Belle Côte Estate Chardonnay

Roasted Poussin with Gigante Beans, Haricot Verts
and Roasted Red Bell Peppers
Peter Michael 2002 Ma Belle–Fille Estate Chardonnay

Rocher aux Amandes
Peter Michael 2002 Les Pavots Estate Bordeaux Blend

160

PETER MICHAEL
WINERY

SIR PETER MICHAEL,
OWNER

12400 IDA CLAYTON ROAD

CALISTOGA, CA 94515

707.942.4459

WWW.PETERMICHAELWINERY.COM

BORN IN 1938, PETER MICHAEL WAS KNIGHTED BY QUEEN ELIZABETH in 1989 in recognition of the economic prosperity spawned by his work in industry and government. Alongside a successful and multi-faceted business career, he has cultivated interests in music and art, as well as wine.

In 1982, Sir Peter Michael established Peter Michael Winery on a square mile of rocky volcanic ridges that form the western face of Mount St. Helena in Sonoma County. From the beginning, his winegrowing philosophy was modeled on the French tradition with a few modern influences—one, the vineyard "terroir" or site would be the single most important feature; two, the wines would be elegant rather than overstated; and three, there would be a 100-year commitment to the development of a great estate.

Peter Michael Winery specializes in only single-vineyard designated wines produced from premium hillside vineyards. Each wine reflects the unique characteristics of its terroir. Traditional winemaking techniques such as French oak aging, a weekly "bâtonnage" (stirring while in barrel) and native fermentations are supplemented by new traditions. For example, to create the desired humidity found in underground caves, they installed a misting system in the barrel aging room. They also designed a hand sorting system to ensure that only fully ripened, whole grape clusters make it into the wine press.

To drink a Peter Michael wine is to experience the flavor and aromas of a vineyard. At Peter Michael, winemaking serves exclusively to preserve the quintessential character and flavor of each vineyard. This ensures that whatever the vineyard gives becomes the wine you enjoy.

Beet Carpaccio with Marinated Rock Shrimp

Dungeness Crab Cakes with Saffron Aioli

Roasted Liberty Farms Duck with Huckleberry Jus

Scharffenberger Flourless Chocolate Cake

One Market

ONE MARKET
MARK DOMMEN,
EXECUTIVE CHEF

1 MARKET STREET

SAN FRANCISCO, CA 94105

415.777.5577

WWW.ONEMARKET.COM

OVERLOOKING THE NEW FERRY BUILDING MARKETPLACE AND BAY BRIDGE, One Market is proud to be located in what has become known as the culinary heart of San Francisco, just steps from the Financial District, Union Square and Moscone Center. The dining room is grand yet inviting with well-spaced tables, deep booths, an exhibition kitchen and picture perfect views of the Bay Bridge, Ferry Building and Embarcadero. A private chef's table in the kitchen provides up to seven guests a rare glimpse of a professional kitchen in action. The lively and casual bar and lounge welcome guests with James Stagg's mural of the Marin Farmers' Market, an extensive wine and spirits selection, and fresh fruit drinks.

Under nationally acclaimed Chef Mark Dommen, the menu changes with the seasons—or even the day, depending on the freshest ingredients available—to highlight the best of local fish and shellfish, produce, meats, poultry, game and other products delivered fresh from local and national artisans and producers. The menu is complemented by a renowned all-American wine list and served by a top-notch staff (interest was so intense that 1,500 people were interviewed for the 125 opening positions!). There's little wonder why the restaurant has been packed from the first day.

Beet Carpaccio with Marinated Rock Shrimp

3 LARGE OR 4 MEDIUM RED BEETS
1 GALLON WATER
2 CUPS RED WINE VINEGAR
1 CUP FINE SEA SALT
1 CUP SUGAR
3" PIECE OF GINGER
1 SHALLOT
1 CUP GRAPESEED OIL
2 TBSP MIRIN
1 TBSP CHAMPAGNE VINEGAR
1/2 TSP SEA SALT
1/4 TSP SUGAR
8 OZ ROCK SHRIMP
FRESH GROUND PEPPER
3 FRENCH BREAKFAST RADISHES
1 4 OZ PKG DAIKON SPROUTS

SERVES 6

Wash the beets and place in a saucepan large enough to fit the water, red wine vinegar, 1 cup of salt and 1 cup of sugar. Bring to a boil. Turn down to a simmer. Cook until the beets are soft and a toothpick can easily be inserted, approximately 1 to 1 1/2 hours depending on size. If the water level reduces below the beets, add more water to the pot until the beets are covered. When cooked, remove from the water and allow to cool.

Peel the ginger. Using a mandoline, slice 18 very thin pieces lengthwise. There should be a small piece of ginger left which should be set aside for later use. In a small saucepan, heat the grapeseed oil to 250°. Add the ginger, fry until golden brown. Remove the ginger from the oil and place onto a paper towel. Sprinkle with salt. Set aside. Allow the oil to cool. It will have acquired a nice ginger flavor and you will use most of it in the other preparations for this dish. Refrigerate the remainder and use for other dishes.

Place the peeled shallot and leftover ginger into a blender with the mirin, champagne vinegar, 1/2 tsp salt and the 1/4 tsp sugar. While blending, slowly add 1/4 cup of the reserved ginger-flavored grapeseed oil. When the oil is incorporated, check the seasoning. Adjust as necessary. Strain through a fine mesh strainer. Set aside.

Heat 1/4 cup of the ginger-flavored grapeseed oil in a medium sauté pan over moderate heat. Season the rock shrimp with salt and freshly ground pepper. Add to the hot sauté pan. Cook the rock shrimp until just barely opaque in the center. Remove to a bowl. Once cool, marinate the rock shrimp with half the ginger vinaigrette. Set aside until ready to use.

ASSEMBLY

Peel the beets. Use the mandoline to slice into paper thin pieces. Arrange directly onto 6 plates in a nice even layer. Brush the top of the beets with the remaining vinaigrette. Sprinkle lightly with salt and pepper. Divide the rock shrimp among the 6 plates and scatter on top of the beets. Thinly slice the radishes using a mandoline. Divide among the 6 plates and scatter on top of the beets and shrimp. Finish by scattering the daikon sprouts on top.

Dungeness Crab Cakes

2 LBS WHOLE DUNGENESS CRAB
(OR SUBSTITUTE 10-12 OZ OF
CLEANED CRABMEAT)
3 OZ FRESH SCALLOPS
1/2 TSP SEA SALT
4 OZ HEAVY CREAM
2 TBSP DIJON MUSTARD
1 TSP CILANTRO, CHOPPED
SEA SALT
FRESH GROUND WHITE PEPPER
PINCH CAYENNE PEPPER
1/4 CUP GRAPESEED OIL

Crack and clean the whole crab. Remove all shells and keep only the meat. Place the crabmeat into a mixing bowl. Refrigerate. A 2 lb crab should yield approximately 10 to 12 oz of cleaned crabmeat.

Place scallops into a blender with 1/2 tsp of salt and a pinch of fresh ground white pepper. Turn on the blender. Slowly add heavy cream in a steady stream. Stop the blender. Scrape down the sides of the blender with a rubber spatula. Blend the mixture 1 more time to make sure the scallop mousse is a nice homogeneous mixture. Set aside.

In the mixing bowl with the crab, add the Dijon mustard and the cilantro. Lightly toss the crab to evenly disperse the ingredients. Add the scallop mousse. Mix lightly; do not break up the crab. Evenly mix mousse throughout the crab. Season to taste with sea salt, fresh ground white pepper and a pinch of cayenne. Crab mixture will keep in refrigerator if made in advance.

Form the cakes into a free form shape about 1 oz each. Place on a lightly oiled baking dish.

Before serving, turn the broiler on high and allow it to heat up. Lightly brush the tops of the crab cakes with grapeseed oil. Place under the broiler for 3 to 5 minutes until they begin to lightly brown on top and are heated through. Remove from the broiler. With a spatula, place on a serving platter or individual plates. Serve with Saffron Aioli.

 SAFFRON AIOLI

1 EGG YOLK
2 TBSP DIJON MUSTARD
1 TSP CHAMPAGNE VINEGAR
1/2 TSP FRESH SQUEEZED LEMON JUICE
1/8 TSP SAFFRON
1/4 TSP SEA SALT
PINCH CAYENNE
1/2 CUP GRAPESEED OIL

❖ Place all ingredients into a blender except the grapeseed oil. Turn on the blender. Slowly add grapeseed oil in a slow steady stream until all the oil is incorporated and nicely emulsified. Adjust seasoning to taste. Refrigerate until ready to use.

165

Roasted Liberty Farms Duck with Huckleberry Jus

2 6 LB LIBERTY FARMS DUCKS
6 CUPS DUCK FAT (RENDERED)
SEA SALT
CRACKED BLACK PEPPER
FRESH GROUND BLACK PEPPER
1/2 BUNCH SAGE
1 BUNCH THYME
2 BAY LEAVES
12 CLOVES GARLIC
1 LB CAUL FAT
3 MEDIUM TURNIPS
2 TBSP BUTTER
1 CUP CREAM
1 1/2 SPRIGS ROSEMARY
2 BUNCHES SWISS CHARD
1 CUP HUCKLEBERRY DUCK JUS

❦ HUCKLEBERRY DUCK JUS
DUCK BONES, COARSELY CHOPPED INTO SMALL PIECES
2 ONIONS, COARSELY CHOPPED
2 CARROTS, COARSELY CHOPPED
2 RIBS OF CELERY, COARSELY CHOPPED
1 TBSP TOMATO PASTE
2 CUPS RED WINE
2 CUPS PORT WINE
1 1/2 QTS CHICKEN STOCK
3 SPRIGS THYME
1/2 SPRIG ROSEMARY
2 FRESH BAY LEAVES
2 OZ HUCKLEBERRIES

SERVES 6

Debone the ducks. Remove the breasts and legs from the carcasses (or ask your butcher to). Reserve carcasses for the duck jus. Preheat your oven to 250°. Season the duck legs with sea salt and cracked black pepper. Let sit for 2 hours allowing the salt to penetrate the meat.

Place the duck legs and rendered duck fat into a large saucepan. Add half of the thyme, the garlic cloves, the bay leaf and 1 sprig of the rosemary. Bring the duck fat and legs to a simmer. Cover. Place in the oven for approximately 1 1/2 to 2 hours until the duck meat is soft and falling away from the bones.

Gently remove the duck legs from the fat. Discard the herbs. Allow the legs to cool. When cooled enough to handle, remove the meat from the bones and skin. Reserve the meat and throw away the rest. Place the duck leg meat into a bowl. Season with chopped thyme, chopped sage, fresh ground pepper and sea salt to taste. Divide the duck leg meat into 6 even portions. Spread the caul fat out onto a cutting board. Carefully wrap the individual leg portions. Shape them into a disk.

Peel the turnips. Cut into approximately 3/8" cubes. In a small pot, melt the butter. Add the chopped turnips. Cook without giving them any color. Add the cream and rosemary. Bring to a boil. Turn down to a simmer. Continue to cook the turnips until the cream has reduced and the turnips are soft. Season to taste with salt and freshly ground pepper.

Remove the rosemary from the turnips. Transfer the mixture to a blender. Blend to a fine purée. Season to taste. Reserve, keeping hot.

Wash the swiss chard, removing the stems. Coarsely chop it into manageable pieces. (The stems can be pickled and added back to the chard when cooked or you can throw them out.) In a large sauté pan, heat 1 tbsp of butter. Add the swiss chard. Cook until soft. If necessary, add a few drops of water to the chard while cooking to create a little steam. This will help it wilt and cook faster. Season to taste with salt and pepper.

Season the duck breasts with salt and pepper. Place skin side down in a heavy bottom skillet. Cook at low temperature on top of the stove. Render most of the fat from the skin. This can take 15 minutes or so. When the skin looks crispy, turn up the heat. Flip over the breast to get a nice sear on the flesh side. Cook until medium rare. Remove from the pan. Allow to rest for at least 10 minutes in a warm place.

In another heavy bottom skillet over medium to high heat, place 2 tbsp duck fat from the confit. Sear the duck confit disks until golden brown.

✤ In a large heavy bottom pot over medium to high heat, add the duck bones. Allow to brown evenly by stirring continuously. When the bones are nice and brown, strain off excess fat that has rendered out from the bones. Add the chopped vegetables to the pan. Continue to brown the vegetables and the bones. When the vegetables are nice and brown, add the tomato paste. Gently cook for 2 more minutes.

Deglaze the pot with the red wine and port wine. Reduce until almost dry. Cover with the chicken stock. Add the rest of the ingredients. Bring to a boil. Turn down until it is barely simmering. Cook for 2 1/2 to 3 hours. Strain through a fine mesh strainer or cheesecloth. Skim off excess fat that may rise to the surface. Once degreased, place back on the stove. Reduce over high heat until it coats the back of a sauce spoon. Yields approximately 1 to 2 cups of duck jus.

When ready to serve, bring the duck jus to a boil in a small saucepan. Turn the flame low. Add the huckleberries. Check the seasoning.

ASSEMBLY

Divide the turnip purée evenly among 6 plates. Place the sautéed chard on top of the turnip purée. Place a duck confit disk on top. Slice the duck breasts and divide among the 6 plates, laying it on top of the duck leg disk. Drizzle the Huckleberry Duck Jus on top.

Scharffenberger Flourless Chocolate Cake

SERVES 10

10 1/2 OZ BITTERSWEET CHOCOLATE
5 OZ UNSALTED BUTTER
6 EXTRA LARGE EGGS, SEPARATED
4 1/2 OZ SUGAR, DIVIDED IN HALF
2 TSP PURE VANILLA EXTRACT OR
LIQUEUR OF CHOICE
PINCH OF SALT
1/4 TSP CREAM OF TARTAR

Preheat oven to 325°. Butter a 9" spring form pan and set aside. Melt chocolate and butter together in a bain marie. Remove and let cool slightly. Whip egg yolks with half of sugar, salt and vanilla extract (or liqueur) in the bowl of a standing mixer until thick, billowy and tripled in volume.

In a clean bowl, whip egg whites until frothy. Add cream of tartar. Continue whipping until soft peaks form. Add sugar in 2 additions. Mix only until firm peaks form. Fold yolk mixture into chocolate mixture gently but quickly, leaving the mixture streaky (do not mix completely). Fold in egg whites, careful not to deflate.

Pour batter into prepared pan. Place in preheated oven. Bake until slightly souffléd and no longer liquid in center. Cool before unmolding.

Serve with seasonal fruit tossed in honey and your favorite liqueur.

Wine Pairing

Beet Carpaccio with Marinated Rock Shrimp
Qupé 2004 Marsanne

Dungeness Crab Cakes with Saffron Aioli
Qupé 2003 Rousanne,
Bien Nacido Hillside Estate

Roasted Liberty Farms Duck with Huckleberry Jus
Qupé 2003 Los Olivos Cuvée

Scharffenberger Flourless Chocolate Cake
Qupé 2003 Syrah,
Bien Nacido Vineyard

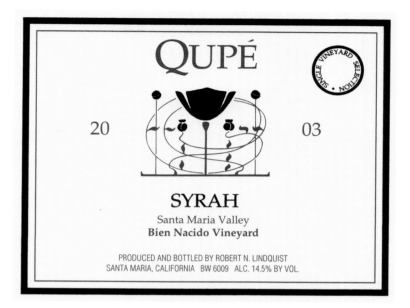

QUPÉ

20 — 03

SYRAH

Santa Maria Valley
Bien Nacido Vineyard

PRODUCED AND BOTTLED BY ROBERT N. LINDQUIST
SANTA MARIA, CALIFORNIA BW 6009 ALC. 14.5% BY VOL.

SINGLE VINEYARD SELECTION

QUPÉ
WINE CELLARS

Bob Lindquist,
Owner and Winemaker

PO BOX 440

LOS OLIVOS, CA 93441

805.937.9801

WWW.QUPE.COM

While managing a retail shop in Los Olivos, Bob's career took what some thought to be a bad hop. He got fired for attending a Kinks concert against the wishes of the shop owner. But fate intervened and he was immediately hired as Zaca Mesa Winery's first tour guide—a job that included cellar work. There he met winemakers Ken Brown and Jim Clendenen who taught Bob the basics of winemaking and inspired him to become a winemaker himself. He founded Qupé in 1982.

He continued his work at Zaca Mesa to provide what he needed for Qupé—he bought barrels and grapes and traded his services for the loan of the equipment in the cellar. His first vintage he produced Syrah, Chardonnay and a Rosé of Pinot Noir. Bob's love of the assertive and complex wines of the Rhône Valley led him to focus Qupé on the production of Rhône varietals, particularly Syrah.

In 1989 Bob joined forces with his mentor and friend Jim Clendenen of Au Bon Climat. Together they built a shared winery in the Bien Nacido Vineyard in Santa Maria, California. Once a year during harvest, visiting winemakers and wine professionals of various nationalities and backgrounds join Bob and Jim at the winery to share techniques and ideas.

Qupé also farms the 14-acre organic Ibarra-Young Vineyard in Los Olivos, California, and Bob is involved in Verdad, a winery dedicated to Spanish grape varieties produced by his wife Louisa. Bob and Louisa recently purchased an 80-acre vineyard site in the Edna Valley where they will grow their grapes and build a home.

Asparagi all Griglia con Bagna Brusca

Fedelini con Granchio

Pollo alla Marsala con Spinaci Siciliani

Panna Cotta

Palio d'Asti
Gianni Fassio,
Founder
Daniel Scherotter,
Executive Chef
and Partner

640 sacramento street

san francisco, ca 94111

415.395.9800

www.paliodasti.com

You want authentic Italian cuisine—you go to Palio d'Asti. Palio d'Asti's success in fostering the renaissance of true Italian food in San Francisco has garnered its founder, Gianni Fassio, a civic knighthood in Italy as well as frequent recognition by the American press. His chef and partner, Daniel Scherotter, worked in Bologna, Italy for two years before coming to San Francisco where he attended the California Culinary Academy. After working under top chefs and working a year at Palio, in 1999, Fassio brought Scherotter back as the executive chef to garner yet another 3 star review and eventually become a partner.

Scherotter, who speaks Italian, shares Fassio's vision and passion for the inexhaustible riches of Italy's table. Though they both love the extravagant food of northern Italy, Scherotter eloped to Sicily in 2003 and has a fondness for that island's exotic fusion cuisine which he frequently serves. His menu reflects the refined north in the fall and winter, the exuberant south in the summer and the green center in spring. Likewise, the wine list focuses on Italy and California's best producers, both well-known and as yet undiscovered. Fassio and Scherotter taste thousands of wines a year to offer excellent pairings and values to go with Scherotter's food.

Palio's professional staff is impeccable and its hostess, Evelyn Wu, has been written up by Zagat as the best hostess in San Francisco. Come enjoy the best of Italy in San Francisco's Financial District!

Asparagi all Griglia con Bagna Brusca

This is a classic springtime dish throughout northern Italy with two of the most recognizable symbols of the season: eggs and asparagus. This sauce is also good on fish and other vegetables.

1 1/2 LB MEDIUM ASPARAGUS

6 EGGS

1 CUP UNFILTERED EXTRA VIRGIN OLIVE OIL

2 TBSP CAPERS, CHOPPED

12 WHITE ANCHOVY FILETS, CHOPPED

1 BUNCH ITALIAN FLAT LEAF PARSLEY, CHOPPED

6 LEMONS, ZEST AND JUICE SEPARATED

COARSE GRAIN KOSHER SALT (QUANTO BASTA)

SERVES 4 TO 6

Bring a large pot of salted water to a boil. Cut off woody ends of asparagus at an angle. Blanch for 2 minutes or until bright green. Fill bowl with ice water. Remove blanched asparagus and immediately shock in ice water. Hard boil eggs in asparagus water for 7 minutes, and shock.

Chop egg yolks and whites separately. If white anchovies are unavailable, submerge fresh raw anchovies in lemon juice and salt for approximately 1 hour at room temperature. Peel cured meat from the bone. If fresh anchovies are unavailable, take canned anchovies and soak in milk for 1 hour and then lemon juice for another hour. Combine all dry ingredients and salt. Saturate with oil and fold together gently with a rubber spatula. Pour in 4 oz of lemon juice. Mix and taste for lemon and salt.

Lightly oil asparagus. Grill, being careful not to let flames lick the oil. Roll around until lightly browned. Place on a platter. Salt, sauce and serve.

Fedelini con Granchio

❖ This is my best selling pasta dish day in and day out and shows just how versatile tomato sauce can be. Other types of crabmeat will work, but here in San Francisco we are truly blessed by the Dungeness. Don't omit the breadcrumbs, they are the best part.

Sweat vegetables until limp but not browned. Add canned tomatoes and slowly bring to a boil, stirring constantly. Reduce to a simmer and let cook 1 hour or until just thickened. Throw in basil leaves and purée with an immersion blender. Cool down rapidly and refrigerate.

❖ Cut the crusts off the bread. Cut into croutons. Let dry on a cookie sheet in oven at 200° until hard but not brown. Grind up the bread in a food processor. Sift out the dust so you have fairly even-sized pieces. Put a large skillet over medium heat. Cover the bottom of the pan with olive oil. Add the breadcrumbs and more oil. Toast until golden, stirring and tossing constantly. When done, let cool on a cookie sheet. Store in sealed container at room temperature. Lasts for weeks.

❖ Bring a large pot of heavily salted water to a boil. Drop in pasta and stir. Never put oil in the water. Put garlic and oil in a large, wide saucepan and heat up. When you can smell the garlic, but long before it browns, add the crab, dry oregano and chili flakes. Stir until it begins to sizzle. Add the wine. Reduce. Add the tomato sauce. Bring to a rapid boil and reduce slightly to emulsify. Before pasta is done and while it is still crunchy, remove from water. Add to sauce and stir. Let the pasta soak in the sauce. Season with salt and chili flakes to taste. If it dries out before the pasta is cooked, add a little pasta water. Stir in parsley. There should be no excess tomato water. Serve on plates or bowls and top with breadcrumbs.

❖ **TOMATO SAUCE**

1 SMALL CAN OF SAN MARZANO ITALIAN TOMATOES
1 YELLOW ONION, SLICED
2 CELERY STALKS, CHOPPED
6 GARLIC CLOVES
2 OZ OLIVE OIL
1 BUNCH BASIL

❖ **BREADCRUMBS**

LARGE OLD SOURDOUGH LOAF
EXTRA VIRGIN OLIVE OIL

❖ **PASTA**

1 1/2 LB DI CECCO FEDELINI PASTA OR SPAGHETTINI
4 OZ OLIVE OIL
1 TBSP GARLIC, CHOPPED
1 PINT TOMATO SAUCE
1 LB FRESH PICKED DUNGENESS CRAB MEAT
6 OZ WHITE WINE
2 TSP DRY OREGANO
1 BUNCH ITALIAN PARSLEY, CHOPPED
CHILI FLAKES TO TASTE
SALT TO TASTE
BREADCRUMBS

173

Pollo alla Marsala con Spinaci Siciliani

*Chicken Marsala with Sicilian Spinach is a worldwide favorite.
I've lightened this dish up considerably from the way I was taught to make it.*

6 SMALL CHICKEN BREASTS WITH SKIN
(ADD WINGS FOR A NICE TOUCH)
2 LB CLEAN BABY SPINACH
4 OZ PINE NUTS
3 OZ SULTANA (GOLDEN) RAISINS
1 TBSP TOMATO PASTE
1 TBSP GARLIC, CHOPPED
2 TBSP SHALLOTS, CHOPPED
1 PINT SWEET MARSALA
1 PINT CHICKEN STOCK,
PUT PARMESAN RINDS IN YOUR STOCK
8 OZ SWEET BUTTER
2 OZ GRAPE SEED OIL OR CANOLA OIL
SALT

SERVES 4 TO 6

Heat the oven to 500°.

Using heavy-duty zip-lock bags, pound the chicken breasts so they are of equal thickness. Heat up the raisins in Marsala until they are tender. Separate and set aside.

Use 2 oz of the butter to toast the pine nuts. Set aside. Heat up a large, heavy, thick-bottomed skillet with grape seed oil. When it's about to start smoking, salt the skin sides of the chicken breasts and carefully place in the oil. Shake the pan to prevent sticking. Turn heat to medium. Remove chicken breasts to a cookie sheet when brown. Only put in enough breasts to cover the bottom of the skillet. When all breasts are browned on the skin side and moved to the cookie sheet, place in the bottom rack of the oven.

Pour off excess oil in the skillet. Add 2 oz of butter and the shallots, scraping bottom with a wooden spoon. When caramelly, add the Marsala (not the raisins) and expect a flame. Reduce to a glaze. Add the tomato paste and dissolve. Add the chicken stock and reduce. Add remainder of the butter until slightly thickened. Salt to taste.

In a wok or pot large enough to hold all the spinach, put the pine nuts, their butter and the garlic in the pot and turn to medium. When they start to boil, add the spinach and raisins. Salt to taste. Stir frequently until spinach is just cooked. Put on a platter. Place chicken breasts on top of spinach. Pour sauce over the breasts.

174

Panna Cotta

1 1/2 CUPS HEAVY CREAM
1 CUP BUTTERMILK
1/2 VANILLA BEAN
6 OZ SUGAR
5 SHEETS GELATIN
5 LEMON PEELS (USE A POTATO PEELER)

Literally "cooked cream," this is an eggless custard that's lighter than crème brulee and a perfect dessert with fresh berries, toasted nuts and a variety of spices. Prepare it a day ahead of time. Use fun-shaped 3 to 4 oz plastic molds (we use a cone shape) to add drama to the presentation.

Bring cream and sugar to a boil with the vanilla bean and lemon peel. Soften the gelatin separately in a bit of the cream and re-add. Allow to cool to just warm. Add buttermilk and strain. Pour into plastic molds and refrigerate overnight. Pop out onto cold plates when ready to serve. Decorate with your choice of seasonal fruits and nuts. Honey is also good.

Wine Pairing

Asparagi all Griglia con Bagna Brusca
2004 Arneis

Fedelini con Granchio
2003 Sangiovese

Pallo alla Marsala con Spinaci Siciliani
2003 Old Vine Zinfandel

Panna Cotta
2003 Keyhole Ranch Pinot Noir

SEGHESIO FAMILY VINEYARDS WAS THE DREAM OF YOUNG ITALIAN immigrants Edoardo and Angela Seghesio who met while each worked at the Italian Swiss Colony Winery in northern Sonoma County. In 1895, the couple purchased the original family home and a 56-acre ranch in Alexander Valley. Edoardo continued as winemaker at Italian Swiss Colony until 1902 when he completed his dream—construction of Seghesio Winery.

That passion to grow some of the finest wine grapes in California and to produce wines worthy of a friend's table lives on 100 years and 400 acres later in Edoardo and Angela Seghesio's grandchildren.

Today, third and fourth generation Seghesio family members passionately work to evolve and improve upon the treasure of the vineyards they have been given. They have gained a reputation for producing some of the finest Zinfandels in the world, several from vineyards planted over 100 years ago. They continue to honor their heritage with an award-winning and food-loving offering of Italian varietals.

Evidence of the Seghesio family's talent for blending the past and the future of California's wine industry is evident at their Healdsburg winery where visitors sip new world-class wines in a cellar dating back to 1895.

SEGHESIO
FAMILY VINEYARDS

SEGHESIO FAMILY,
OWNERS≥≥

14730 GROVE STREET

HEALDSBURG, CA 95448

707.433.3579

WWW.SEGHESIO.COM

Ahi Tuna Carpaccio with Watercress, Fennel and Citrus Salad

Spinach Ricotta Gnocchi

Spit-roasted Pork Loin with White Beans all' Uccelletto

Panna Cotta with Huckleberry Sauce

Poggio

POGGIO
LARRY MINDEL,
OWNER
UMBERTO GIBIN,
MANAGING PARTNER
CHRIS FERNANDEZ,
EXECUTIVE CHEF
AND PARTNER

777 BRIDGEWAY
SAUSALITO, CA 94965
415.332.7771
WWW.POGGIOTRATTORIA.COM

POGGIO IS A CLASSIC ITALIAN TRATTORIA WITH COMFORTABLE neighborhood charm and destination-caliber cuisine. Partners Umberto Gibin, Larry Mindel and Chris Fernandez have tapped the essence of a trattoria. It may turn out to be the world's most perfect Italian restaurant outside of Italy. Honored as one of America's best new restaurants by John Mariani in the November 2004 edition of *Esquire*, as well as by the *San Francisco Chronicle* and *San Francisco Examiner*, the restaurant is at once quintessentially Italian and at ease in its Northern California locale. Using the best available local ingredients and property-grown herbs and vegetables, the daily changing menu features soulful classics of Northern Italy, simply and earnestly prepared.

The main dining room is capped by graceful Tuscan arches and accented in polished mahogany paneling. A floor-to-ceiling wine cabinet displays a vast collection of vintages, mostly from Italy, and a handful of wines from Umberto and Larry's California *amici della famiglia*. At the center of the room is an exhibition kitchen, set like a stage for the chefs to carry out their culinary performances. A wood-burning rotisserie provides rustic warmth throughout the space.

The overall dynamic is one of neighborly charm and great food—the kind of place people will drive for miles to visit, and locals will visit several times a month. "I love this idea of the 'third place' in a person's social life being the restaurant," says Larry. "You've got the home, the workplace and the neighborhood trattoria as primary places in a person's life for social interaction. That's the style in which we've created Poggio."

Ahi Tuna Carpaccio with Watercress, Fennel and Citrus Salad

8-10 OZ CENTER CUT AHI TUNA LOIN

SERVES 4

Slice the tuna very thin. Place between parchment paper. Lightly pound the tuna to enlarge the pieces and make very thin. Place the thin tuna on plates. Wrap with plastic wrap and refrigerate until ready to use.

✤ **DRESSING**
2 SHALLOTS, MINCED
4 TBSP CHAMPAGNE VINEGAR
6 TBSP EXTRA VIRGIN OLIVE OIL
SEA SALT

✤ Place the minced shallots in a bowl with the champagne vinegar. Let set for 30 minutes. Whisk in the extra virgin olive oil and salt.

✤ **SALAD**
1 BUNCH WATERCRESS
1 RED ONION
1 BULB FENNEL
3-4 PIECES OF CITRUS, EITHER MANDARIN ORANGE, TANGERINE OR BLOOD ORANGE

✤ Wash and drain the watercress. Peel and slice the red onion into paper-thin rings. Set aside. Slice the fennel paper thin and set aside. Peel the citrus skin with a knife and then slice the citrus into thin wheels.

ASSEMBLY

Dress the tuna carpaccio with a spoonful of the dressing and a pinch of sea salt. Dress the watercress, red onion, fennel and citrus wheels with the dressing and place on top of the carpaccio.

Spinach Ricotta Gnocchi

SERVES 4

1/2 LB RICOTTA CHEESE (DRAINED IN
CHEESECLOTH OVERNIGHT)

1/4 LB SAVOY SPINACH

1 QT WATER

2 OZ POTATO STARCH

1 TBSP DEHYDRATED POTATO

2 TBSP FLOUR

1 TBSP PARMESAN CHEESE

1 EGG

PINCH OF GROUND NUTMEG

SALT TO TASTE

2 CUPS FLOUR

Place the ricotta in a strainer lined with cheesecloth. Let sit overnight to remove excess liquid. Bring the water to a boil. Add the spinach and boil for 30 seconds. Strain the spinach and place it on a sheet pan lined with parchment paper. Place the spinach in the refrigerator to cool. Once cooled, squeeze out all of the excess water from the spinach. Chop the spinach as fine as you can on a cutting board. The finer the better. Place the chopped spinach, ricotta, Parmesan, egg, nutmeg and a pinch of salt in a large mixing bowl. Mix until the spinach has been evenly distributed. Add the potato starch, dehydrated potato and 2 tbsp of flour to bind the mixture.

To test the consistency and flavor of the gnocchi, bring a small pot of water to a boil. Drop in a spoon-size piece of gnocchi. If the gnocchi is too wet and falls apart, you will need to add another egg and some flour. (The key to this gnocchi is to add the minimum amount of binder so that the gnocchi are as light as possible). Place a large pot on the stove with plenty of water to boil the gnocchi. Bring the water up to a boil and turn down until you are ready to cook the gnocchi.

Place the remaining 2 cups of flour in a long baking pan. Place the gnocchi mixture into a piping bag with a large straight tip about 1/2" in diameter. Pipe the gnocchi mixture in a long line directly into the flour, as if you were making a long snake-like piece. You can make a couple of lines like this in the flour.

With a knife or straight bench scraper, cut the gnocchi into the flour to 1" pieces. With your hands, gently pick the gnocchi out of the flour and place directly into the boiling salted water. You will want to cook the gnocchi for at least 5 minutes or until they float for 2 minutes. Remove from the water. Now you can either Serve immediately or hold these gnocch for later use. If you plan to hold the gnocchi, place the cooked gnocchi onto a lightly oiled sheet pan and place in the refrigerator. Once cooled, the gnocchi can be placed into an airtight container until you are ready to use it. The gnocchi can then be reheated in boiling water for 4 to 5 minutes.

181

Spit-roasted Pork Loin with White Beans all' Uccelletto

1 PORK LOIN, BONE ON
1 BUNCH SAGE, LEAVES PICKED
1 BUNCH ROSEMARY, LEAVES PICKED
1 TSP CHILI FLAKES
SALT AND PEPPER TO TASTE

✤ WHITE BEANS ALL'
"UCCELLETTO" (IN THE
STYLE OF LITTLE BIRDS)
6 CUPS COOKED CANNELLINI BEANS
AND THEIR LIQUID
2 TBSP EXTRA VIRGIN OLIVE OIL
1/2 CUP YELLOW ONION, DICED
3 CLOVES GARLIC, SLICED
2 ROSEMARY BRANCHES
6-8 SAGE LEAVES
2 OZ PROSCIUTTO
2 TBSP TOMATO PASTE
SALT
OLIVE OIL

SERVES 6

First, prepare the pork loin. Cut down the back of the loin along the rib bones to separate the meat from the bones. Do not completely remove the bones. Place the sage leaves, rosemary leaves, chili flakes, salt and pepper between the loin and the bones. Bring back the bones and the loin and tie the roast with a butcher's tie. Season the outside of the roast with salt and pepper. Set aside until ready to roast. This may be done up to 2 days prior to roasting. It is preferred to do it at least 1 day prior so that the herbs can flavor the meat.

To cook the pork loin if using a rotisserie
Place the pork on the spit and roast over a high flame for 30 to 40 minutes or until the roast reaches 130°.

To cook the pork loin if using an oven
Place the roast in a roasting pan and roast at 450° for 10 minutes. Reduce heat to 350° and roast for 30 to 40 more minutes until the temperature is 130°. Remove the roast and allow it to rest for 10 to 15 minutes.

✤ Heat the olive oil in a medium saucepan over a low flame. Add the onion, garlic, rosemary and sage and sweat until the onions are soft and translucent. Add the beans and some of the juice, reserving some of the juice in case the beans need moisture at the end of cooking. Add the prosciutto and the tomato paste, achieving a dark orange color. Season with salt. Simmer for up to 2 hours to fully flavor the beans.

ASSEMBLY

Place the warm beans on a plate or a platter. Remove the string and the bones from the pork roast. Thinly slice the roast and place next to the beans. Cut the rib bones and place 1 bone on each plate. Garnish the roast with a small watercress salad and a drizzle of fine olive oil.

182

Panna Cotta with Huckleberry Sauce

SERVES 4 ❧ **PANNA COTTA**

1 1/2 CUPS CREAM

1/2 CUP MILK

2 VANILLA BEANS

2 GELATIN SHEETS

3 TBSP SUGAR

❧ In a medium saucepan, scald the cream, milk and vanilla beans. Add the sugar. Stir to dissolve. Remove from heat and cool for 30 minutes to infuse the vanilla. Soften the gelatin in a small amount of cold water for about 5 minutes. Add to the warm milk mixture. Cool the mixture slightly over an ice water bath until it reaches body temperature. Fill coffee cups or soufflé ramekins about 2/3 full. Place in refrigerator to chill and set.

❧ **HUCKLEBERRY SAUCE**

1 1/2 CUPS SUGAR

2 LBS HUCKLEBERRIES

WHIPPED CREAM TO TOP

❧ Place the huckleberries and sugar in a medium saucepot. Simmer for 1 to 2 hours or until the sauce becomes thick. Set aside to cool. When cool, place the sauce in a blender and purée. Pass through a fine mesh strainer to remove skins.

ASSEMBLY

Place the Panna Cotta ramekin in a small pan of hot water to soften the gelatin. Invert the ramekin onto a plate. Garnish with the Huckleberry Sauce, a spoonful of whipped cream and some of the huckleberries tossed in sugar.

Wine Pairing

Ahi Tuna Carpaccio
with Watercress, Fennel and Citrus Salad
2002 Estate Chardonnay

Spinach Ricotta Gnocchi
2002 "Dobles Lias" Chardonnay

Spit-roasted Pork Loin
with White Beans all Uccelletto
2002 Estate Pinot Noir

Panna Cotta with Huckleberry Sauce
2002 "Cristina" Pinot Noir

Born in Barcelona, Spain, owner Marimar Torres has been involved in the wine business all her life. Marimar Estate and Don Miguel Vineyard—named after her late father and the patriarch of the Torres' family—are nestled in the rolling hills of western Sonoma County in the Russian River/Green Valley appellation.

The location is a perfect microclimate for growing Chardonnay and Pinot Noir. Only ten miles from the Pacific Ocean and 50 miles north of San Francisco, the site benefits from the sea's cooling breezes and drifting fog. The vineyard is unique to California because of its totally European style, including the high-density planting of 2,000 vines per acre.

April 2003 marked the conversion to all organic farming methods at Marimar Estate's Don Miguel Vineyard. "After experimenting for about four years with a few blocks of vines, we finally decided to make the jump to the entire vineyard," says Marimar Torres. "The whole idea is to create an ideal balance between the vines and nature. The vineyard will be ecologically healthier and the grapes a higher quality. That's our long-term reward." Organic certification is a three-year process, at the end of which a winery can note on the label that its wine is made from organic grapes.

MARIMAR
ESTATE

MARIMAR TORRES,
OWNER

11400 GRATON ROAD

SEBASTOPOL, CA 95472

707.823.4365

WWW.MARIMARESTATE.COM

Seared Mano de Leon Scallops, Baby Spinach and Avocado
with Yuzu and Truffle Vinaigrette

Asparagus "Baklava"

Macadamia Crusted Halibut in Coconut Broth with Braising Greens and Pineapple Chutney

Shortbread with Grand Marnier Soaked Strawberries and Chantilly Cream

SUTRO'S
AT THE CLIFF HOUSE
PATRICK W. CLARK,
CHEF

1090 PT. LOBOS

SAN FRANCISCO, CA 94121

415.386.3330

WWW.CLIFFHOUSE.COM

IF YOU WANT TO EXPERIENCE THE TRUE FLAVOR OF THE NORTHERN California coast, visit Sutro's in the famed Cliff House at Ocean Beach. Perched on the rocky cliffs above the Pacific Ocean, Sutro's provides panoramic views of the Marin coastline, the Sutro Bath ruins and the Farallon Islands.

Originally built in 1863 and renovated in 2004, Sutro's at Cliff House is the place to go for a romantic evening or to entertain (and impress) out-of-town guests. The restaurant's modern décor with its well-spaced tables and upholstered booths lends itself to casual dining and good conversation.

Award winning chef Patrick Clark brings his experience and his California Culinary Academy skills to Sutro's. "We're sitting right on top of the ocean, so seafood is going to play a major role in the menu," says Chef Clark. And indeed, it does. Smoked Bacon Crusted Tasmanian Salmon with Truffled Potatoes and Bloomsdale Spinach, Macadamia Nut Crusted Local Halibut in Coconut Broth, and Sutro's Swordfish are enough to satisfy the heartiest cravings for gifts from the sea. Finish with Pear and Sun Dried Cherry Crêpes with Vanilla Ice Cream and Brown Butter Almond Streusel and you're ready for a visit to the observations decks and a stroll along the cliffs.

"For well prepared American specialties with a view of the sunset that rivals Hawaii, the Cliff House has been a top choice for more than a century." *City Guide Magazine*

Seared Mano de Leon Scallops, Baby Spinach and Avocado with Yuzu and Truffle Vinaigrette

1/2 LB BABY SPINACH
3 AVOCADOS
1 TBSP BLACK SESAME SEEDS

SERVES 6

❖ Place all ingredients in a blender and purée until emulsified.

❖ YUZU AND TRUFFLE VINAIGRETTE

1/4 CUP YUZU JUICE
(AVAILABLE AT ASIAN MARKETS)
1 TSP TRUFFLE OIL
1 TBSP SHALLOTS, CHOPPED
1/2 CUP EXTRA VIRGIN OLIVE OIL
SALT AND BLACK PEPPER TO TASTE

❖ Heat the oil in a large sauté pan and carefully place the scallops in oil. Cook for 1 minute. Add the butter. Spoon the melted butter over the scallops as they cook until a golden brown crust forms on the bottom. Turn the scallops and repeat until scallops are well caramelized and firm to the touch.

❖ SCALLOPS

6 MANO DE LEON SCALLOPS
1 TBSP OLIVE OIL
1 TBSP BUTTER

❖ In a medium saucepan, heat the oil to 400°. Place the noodles in the oil. They will immediately expand. Remove the noodles and place on paper towels to drain excess oil.

188

❖ FRIED RICE NOODLES

1 OZ RICE NOODLES
3 CUPS OIL OR SHORTENING FOR FRYING

ASSEMBLY

Cut the avocados in half. Remove the pit. Spoon the avocados from the skin leaving the halves intact. Place the avocados flat side down and slice them laterally into 1/8" slices, leaving the avocado half in its original shape. Fan the avocado half by placing it near the center of the plate and gently pushing the slices apart. As you expand the avocado slices, gently push them toward the rim of the plate to form a semi-circle.

Season the spinach with salt and pepper and dress with the vinaigrette. Place the spinach in the center of each plate leaving a space opposite the avocado circle for the scallops. Put a few drops of the vinaigrette on the empty part of the plate. Place the scallops on the vinaigrette. Place a small bundle of the fried rice noodles on top. Garnish with black sesame seeds.

Asparagus "Baklava"

❖ ASPARAGUS

2 BUNCHES ASPARAGUS
2 BUNCHES WHITE ASPARAGUS
1 BUNCH PURPLE ASPARAGUS

SERVES 6

❖ Trim the lower stalks off of the white and green asparagus, leaving 3 1/2" spears. In a large stockpot, bring heavily salted water to a boil. Blanch the asparagus for 1 minute and shock in an ice bath. Remove when chilled. Drain off all the excess water.

Using a French bean slicer, shred the purple asparagus. Just before serving, season with salt and pepper and toss with Lemon Vinaigrette.

✤ Mix all ingredients together.

✤ Pick the herbs and take 1/3 of each and chop fine. Reserve the other 2/3 for the herb oil. Place the chèvre and 1/3 of the herbs in an electric stand mixer and whip until light and fluffy. Place the mixture in a large pastry bag with a 1/2" round tip or no tip at all.

Take the remaining herbs and spinach leaves and blanch in salted boiling water for 10 seconds and shock in ice water. Drain the water and place the greens in a dishtowel. Twist from both ends to remove all the water. Place the greens and oil in a blender and blend for 3 to 4 minutes. Strain through a coffee filter, reserving the infused oil and discarding the rest.

✤ Beat the eggs and water. Lay out the first sheet of phyllo dough. (Always keep the remaining phyllo covered as it dries out very quickly.) With a pastry brush, gently brush the egg mixture over the phyllo. Sprinkle with red salt and pepper. Place the next layer of phyllo directly on top of the first and repeat the procedure. Continue until all 4 layers are brushed and seasoned. Using a pizza cutter or a long knife, cut the dough into 20 2"x 3" rectangles. Bake at 350° for about 12 minutes until golden brown.

ASSEMBLY

Place 12 phyllo rectangles on your work surface. Pipe a thin layer of the herbed chèvre onto each rectangle. Place 2 white asparagus and 1 green asparagus on the chèvre on the bottom 6 layers. Place a thin layer of the chèvre on top of the asparagus to act as glue for the phyllo layers. Place 2 green asparagus and 1 white asparagus on the top layer. Place the 6 top layers on the 6 bottom layers and top with the remaining 6 phyllo squares. Gently press the layers together and cut each in half with a serrated knife. Place the 2 halves on a plate. Add a small mound of the asparagus/Lemon Vinaigrette between the halves. Garnish the plate with a few drops of the herb infused oil.

✤ LEMON VINAIGRETTE
1/4 CUP LEMON JUICE
1/2 CUP EXTRA VIRGIN OLIVE OIL
1 TBSP SHALLOTS, MINCED
SALT AND BLACK PEPPER

✤ HERBED CHÈVRE AND HERB INFUSED OIL
1 LB CHÈVRE
2 BUNCHES TARRAGON
2 BUNCHES CHERVIL
1 CUP BABY SPINACH LEAVES
1 1/2 CUP CANOLA OIL

✤ PHYLLO
4 SHEETS PHYLLO DOUGH
2 EGGS
2 TBSP WATER
RED SALT AND BLACK PEPPER

189

Macadamia Crusted Halibut in Coconut Broth with Braising Greens and Pineapple Chutney

6 HALIBUT FILETS
1 CUP JAPANESE BREAD CRUMBS
6 OZ MACADAMIA NUTS
3 TBSP OLIVE OIL

SERVES 6

Place the macadamia nuts in a food processor until well ground. Add the breadcrumbs until mixed. Press the nut mixture onto both sides of the filets. Heat the olive oil in a large sauté pan. Place the filets in the oil. Cook on medium heat until the crust is golden brown. Place the sauté pan in a 400° oven until cooked, approximately 8 minutes.

❖ BRAISING GREENS
1/2 LB BRAISING GREENS
2 TBSP EXTRA VIRGIN OLIVE OIL

❖ Heat olive oil and sauté greens until slightly wilted.

❖ COCONUT BROTH
2 CANS COCONUT MILK
1/2 CUP CREAM
1/2 JALAPEÑO, MINCED
1 STALK LEMON GRASS, CHOPPED
1 LIME, CUT IN HALF
1 TBSP SUGAR

❖ Place all ingredients in a medium saucepan and bring to a boil. Strain.

❖ PINEAPPLE CHUTNEY
1/2 PINEAPPLE, DICED 1/4"
1/4 CUP GOLDEN RAISINS
1 TSP GARLIC, MINCED
1 TSP GINGER, MINCED
1/2 ONION, MINCED
1 TSP MUSTARD SEED
1/2 TSP CHILI FLAKES
1 TBSP SUGAR
1 TBSP CIDER VINEGAR
CHILI OIL GARNISH (OPTIONAL)
PEARL COUSCOUS (OPTIONAL)

❖ Place all ingredients in a large sauté pan and bring mixture to a boil. Reduce heat to medium and reduce until all liquid has evaporated. Stir the mixture constantly until pineapple has taken on a rich caramel color.

ASSEMBLY

Place the greens in the center of a pasta bowl. Pour 2 to 3 oz of the coconut broth in the bottom and drizzle with chili oil. Place the fish atop the greens. Top with a large spoonful of the Pineapple Chutney.

190

Shortbread with Grand Marnier Soaked Strawberries and Chantilly Cream

SERVES 6

❖ Cube the butter. Place all ingredients in a mixer and mix until dough just comes together. Do not over mix. Refrigerate for 1 hour. Roll out the dough to 1/8" thickness.

❖ Brush dough with melted butter. Mix sugar, cinnamon and sliced almonds together in a small bowl. Sprinkle on top of buttered dough. Cut into 18 3"x3" squares. Bake at 350° for 10 minutes or until golden brown.

❖ Wash and quarter the strawberries. Toss in a mixing bowl with Grand Marnier and sugar. Refrigerate.

❖ Place cream and vanilla in a standing mixer and slowly add in the sugar. Whip to medium peaks.

❖ Place the sugar and water in a medium saucepan and reduce by half. Add the blackberries. Purée in a blender. Strain through a fine chinoise. Refrigerate.

ASSEMBLY

On one end of a rectangular plate, place a small mound of strawberries. Place a dollop of chantilly cream in front of the berries. Lean one piece of shortbread against the cream. Continue shingling the layers against the previous one until you have 4 berry and cream mounds with 3 shortbread. Drizzle the Blackberry Coulis around the plate.

 CREAM CHEESE SHORTBREAD
1/2 CUP CREAM CHEESE
3/4 CUP BUTTER
1/4 TSP SALT
3/4 CUP FLOUR

❖ TOPPING
4 OZ SWEET BUTTER, MELTED
1/4 CUP SUGAR
1/8 CUP CINNAMON
1 CUP SLICED ORGANIC ALMONDS
(KNOLL FARM OR OTHER)

❖ STRAWBERRIES
2 BASKETS RIPE ORGANIC STRAWBERRIES
1 TBSP DARK BROWN SUGAR
1 OZ GRAND MARNIER

❖ CHANTILLY CREAM
1 CUP WHIPPING CREAM
1 TSP VANILLA EXTRACT
2 TBSP SUGAR

❖ BLACKBERRY COULIS
1 CUP SUGAR
1 CUP WATER
2 BASKETS BLACKBERRIES

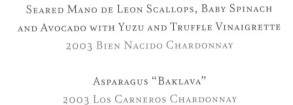

SEARED MANO DE LEON SCALLOPS, BABY SPINACH
AND AVOCADO WITH YUZU AND TRUFFLE VINAIGRETTE
2003 BIEN NACIDO CHARDONNAY

ASPARAGUS "BAKLAVA"
2003 LOS CARNEROS CHARDONNAY

MACADAMIA CRUSTED HALIBUT IN COCONUT BROTH
WITH BRAISING GREENS AND PINEAPPLE CHUTNEY
2001 OAKVILLE ESTATE CABERNET

SHORTBREAD WITH GRAND MARNIER SOAKED STRAWBERRIES
AND CHANTILLY CREAM

**VINE CLIFF
WINERY**

THE SWEENEY FAMILY,
OWNER

7400 SILVERADO TRAIL

NAPA, CA 94558

707.944.1364

WWW.VINECLIFF.COM

VINE CLIFF WINERY HAS MADE A NAME FOR ITSELF IN CONTEMPORARY winemaking in a relatively short period of time. The label, however, has its beginnings in the excitement of the wine boom of the late 1800s and in the history of Napa Valley winemaking.

Vine Cliff Estate is an exquisite mountainside property located on land that was once part of the original George C. Yount Estate. In 1870, noteworthy locals George Burrage and Thomas Tucker purchased the site from the Yount Estate for Vine Cliff Winery. After the deaths of Burrage and Tucker, wealthy San Franciscan John Fry bought the property and immediately set out to achieve his vision for the winery.

The early history of Vine Cliff is contained within a short thirty years. By 1900, phylloxera destroyed the vineyards and existing wine production. Within a few years of Fry's death in 1901, most of the winery structure disappeared with the exception of the stone foundation and the tunnels. Those winery tunnels and the masonry foundation were all that remained when Charles and Nell Sweeney purchased the estate in 1985.

The original winery was resurrected in 1990-1991 with the construction of barrel chais. By 1995, the gravity-fed production facility was completed and now is considered one of the top production facilities in California. In August 2000, 15,000 square feet of barrel-aging caves were completed.

Vine Cliff Winery is a world-class vintner of Cabernet Sauvignon and Chardonnay. Vine Cliff's Cabernet Sauvignon is produced from its estate vineyards in Oakville and its Chardonnay from Vine Cliff vineyards in the Carneros District.

The Sweeney Family continues the vision of Vine Cliff founders Burrage, Tucker and Colonel Fry—to produce outstanding and distinctive wines, and to create a landmark where the incredible beauty of the historic hillside setting can be enjoyed. The legacy of Vine Cliff lives on.

Prawns Mimosa

Steamed Chinese Sea Bass

Grilled Scallops with Thai Chili Sauce

Tropical Fruit Soup with Coconut Foam

Trader Vic's
Pieter Scholte,
Executive Chef

555 Golden Gate Avenue

San Francisco, CA 94102

415.775.6300

www.tradervics.com

Trader Vic's San Francisco marked its triumphant return to San Francisco in November, 2004 when it opened its doors at the former Stars location at Golden Gate and Van Ness Avenues. Completely renovated in the exotic South Seas-style décor known worldwide, Victor "The Trader" Bergeron's legacy and tradition of innovative Island Cuisine and world famous cocktails continues. Trader Vic's visionary combination of quality ingredients and world-class service provides visitors and locals alike with an exotic location in the heart of San Francisco's Civic Center area.

Just five minutes from any of San Francisco's top twenty hotels, there are three private rooms flanking the beautiful Outrigger Room, the main dining room named after the 32 foot outrigger suspended from the high roof ceiling framed by a rock wall lined with orchids. Warm and intimate, private dining rooms are decorated in Island themes and adorned with tiki masks, Polynesian artifacts and unique works of art dedicated to artists and Island royalty. In addition to full catering services with tailored menus, on-site meetings or celebrations can accommodate small sit-down gatherings of eight guests or cocktail parties up to 220. Signature wood-fired Chinese ovens cook mouth-watering seasonal dishes, filling this unique spot with inspiring culinary aromas found only in Trader Vic's award-winning restaurants.

Trader Vic's is truly a world-class addition to San Francisco's world-class reputation as a mecca of fine dining and outstanding service.

Prawns Mimosa

❖ MIMOSA BUTTER

1 LB UNSALTED BUTTER
2 TBSP FRESH LEMON JUICE
1 GARLIC CLOVE, MINCED
1/2 CUP PARSLEY, CHOPPED
1 TBSP WORCESTERSHIRE SAUCE
2 TSP TABASCO
1 CUP PLAIN BREADCRUMBS
SALT AND PEPPER TO TASTE
SALAD GREENS FOR GARNISH

❖ PRAWNS

12 LARGE BLACK TIGER PRAWNS, PEELED
AND DE-VEINED
12 WOODEN SKEWERS, SOAKED IN
WATER
1/2 TBSP SHALLOTS, MINCED
1 TBSP WHITE WINE
1 TBSP BUTTER

SERVES 4

❖ In a food processor, mix all the butter ingredients together well and set aside.

❖ Place 1 prawn on each skewer. In a sauté pan, melt the butter. Add the shallots and cook until soft. Add the prawns to the butter and shallots and cook for 1 minute. Pour the wine into the pan and let simmer for another minute. Remove prawns from the butter mixture and place on a baking sheet. Spread the Mimosa butter on top of the prawns. Place the skewers under the broiler until the prawns have turned golden brown. Place the prawn skewers on a serving plate. Drizzle with the remaining shallot–wine butter. Garnish with salad greens.

196

Steamed Chinese Sea Bass

SERVES 4

Place the fish in an oven-safe dish. Sprinkle the black mushrooms, red bell peppers, garlic and ginger on the fish. Spoon the soy sauce and sesame oil over the fish. Cook the fish for 7 to 8 minutes in a steam kettle. When the fish is finished, place on a serving plate. Spoon the remaining sauce over the fish.

❖ Place the bok choy in boiling salted water for 1 minute. Remove from the water. Place 1 piece on each plate. Place the fish on the bok choy. Top the fish with the mushrooms, bell peppers, garlic and ginger. Sprinkle scallions on the fish and 1 sprig of cilantro. Serve.

4 6 OZ PIECES CHILEAN SEA BASS
10 MEDIUM SHIITAKE MUSHROOMS, SLICED
1 MEDIUM RED BELL PEPPER, JULIENNED
1 GARLIC CLOVE, MINCED
1 PIECE GINGER ROOT, THINLY SLICED
4 TBSP SOY SAUCE
4 TBSP SESAME OIL

❖ GARNISH

4 HEADS BABY BOK CHOY
1 BUNCH SCALLIONS, GREEN PART ONLY, THINLY SLICED
4 SPRIGS CILANTRO

Grilled Scallops with Thai Chili Sauce

10 JUMBO DIVER SCALLOPS

1 TBSP SESAME OIL

SALT AND PEPPER TO TASTE

❖ CHILI SAUCE

10 GARLIC CLOVES

4 RED JALAPENO PEPPERS

3 PIECES SMALL GINGER ROOT

1 PIECE SMALL GALANGAL GINGER

8 KAFFIR LIME LEAVES

3 LEMON GRASS PIECES

1 CUP CILANTRO

1 1/2 CUPS CASTER SUGAR

10 TBSP CIDER VINEGAR

7 TBSP ASIAN FISH SAUCE

2 1/2 TBSP TAMARI SOY SAUCE

❖ GARNISH

4 CUPS WATERCRESS

1/4 CUP OLIVE OIL

1/8 CUP FRESH LEMON JUICE

4 TSP CRÈME FRAICHE OR SOUR CREAM

4 CHERRY TOMATOES

SERVES 1

❖ In a food processor, mix all the ingredients together well. Boil the chili sauce for 5 minutes. Remove from stove and cool at room temperature.

❖ Toss the watercress together with the olive oil and lemon juice. Place 1 cup of salad on the center of each serving plate.

Slice scallops in half and toss with sesame oil, salt and pepper. Place scallops on a hot grill for 1 to 2 minutes. Remove from grill. Place 5 scallop halves around the watercress salad. Spoon the chili sauce on the plate. Top with crème fraiche and 1 cherry tomato.
.

Tropical Fruit Soup with Coconut Foam

SERVES 4

❖ Mix the whipping cream, coconut milk, amaretto and sugar together. Put the cream mixture in a cream whipper. Screw 1 whippet onto the cream whipper and shake well. Keep cold.

❖ In a medium pot, pour all the liquid ingredients along with the ginger and lemongrass. Bring to a boil. Reduce to 4 cups. Add the gelatin. Let it sit for a few minutes. Strain and place in refrigerator for 3 hours.

❖ Cut into small pieces.

ASSEMBLY

Serve 2 scoops of the fruit soup in a deep plate. Sprinkle the fruit on top. Finish with a few small sections of the coconut foam. For a little zing, add a couple of thin slices of jalapeño and a sprig of cilantro.

❖ COCONUT FOAM

2 CUPS WHIPPING CREAM
2 TBSP Amaretto
4 TBSP SUGAR
1 3/4 CUP COCONUT MILK

❖ SOUP

2 CUPS ORANGE JUICE
2 CUPS MANGO JUICE
2 CUPS PASSION FRUIT JUICE
1 1/4 CUP COCONUT MILK
4 PIECES LEMONGRASS
1 PIECE GINGER ROOT
5 LEAVES GELATIN
(PER QT OF JUICE)

❖ FRUIT

1 CAN PEELED LITCHI, DICED
1 RIPE MANGO, DICED
1 RIPE PAPAYA, DICED
4 KUMQUATS, SEEDS REMOVED
1 SMALL PINEAPPLE, DICED
2 PASSION FRUIT, SEEDS REMOVED
JALAPEÑO AND SPRIG OF CILANTRO
FOR GARNISH

199

Wine Pairing

PRAWNS MIMOSA
WENTE VINEYARDS SAUVIGNON BLANC

STEAMED CHINESE SEA BASS
WENTE VINEYARDS RELIZ CREEK RESERVE PINOT NOIR

GRILLED SCALLOPS WITH THAI CHILI SAUCE
WENTE VINEYARDS RIVA RANCH RESERVE CHARDONNAY

TROPICAL FRUIT SOUP WITH COCONUT FOAM
WENTE VINEYARDS RIESLING

200

FOUNDED IN 1883, WENTE VINEYARDS IS California's oldest family owned and continuously operated winery. C. H. Wente learned the art of winemaking from Charles Krug. Recognizing that the warm days, cool nights and gravelly soils of the Livermore Valley were ideal for growing grapes, he purchased 48 acres and planted his vineyards. The winery is now owned and managed by the fourth and fifth generations of the Wente family who continue the tradition of producing excellent wines of distinguished character at an affordable price.

The winery farms nearly 3,000 acres of estate vineyards in the Livermore Valley and Arroyo Seco, two premier Central Coast winegrowing regions.

The Livermore Valley lies fifteen miles east of San Francisco Bay, and is significantly influenced by the moderating effects of the Bay as well as the marine breezes from the Pacific Ocean. Three distinct soil types differentiate the Wentes' Livermore Valley vineyards—deep sandy loam; lean soil with large amounts of gravel and rock; and soil composed of red clay, rock and gravel. These soils, in combination with the micro-climates of the Livermore Valley, create the varying terroir suitable to producing extraordinary wines.

The family's Monterey vineyards are located slightly southwest of Salinas in the Arroyo Seco region. Arroyo Seco is a cooler area with an extended growing season, resulting in wines with concentrated flavors.

The Wente family invites visitors to share wine country experiences at their award-winning Restaurant at Wente Vineyards in the Livermore Valley. Guests can also enjoy Wente Vineyards' Greg Norman-designed golf course, wine country events center, summer concert series and two tasting rooms.

WENTE
VINEYARDS

WENTE FAMILY,
OWNER

5565 TESLA ROAD

LIVERMORE, CA 94550

925.455.2300

WWW.WENTEVINEYARDS.COM

LIQUID AND DRY MEASURES

U.S.			METRIC
1/4 teaspoon			1.23 milliliters
1/2 teaspoon			2.46 milliliters
3/4 teaspoon			3.7 milliliters
1 teaspoon			4.93 milliliters
1 1/4 teaspoons			6.16 milliliters
1 1/2 teaspoons			7.39 milliliters
1 3/4 teaspoons			8.63 milliliters
2 teaspoons			9.86 milliliters
1 tablespoon			14.79 milliliters
2 tablespoons			29.57 milliliters

3 teaspoons	1 tablespoon	1/2 ounce	14.3 grams
2 tablespoons	1/8 cup	1 ounce	28.3 grams
4 tablespoons	1/4 cup	2 ounces	56.7 grams
5 1/3 tablespoons	1/3 cup	2.6 ounces	75.6 grams
8 tablespoons	1/2 cup	4 ounces	113.4 grams
12 tablespoons	3/4 cup	6 ounces	170 grams
16 tablespoons	1 cup	8 ounces	226.8 grams
32 tablespoons	2 cups	16 ounces	453.6 grams
64 tablespoons	4 cups	32 ounces	907.2 grams

1 oz.			30 milliliters
16 oz	1 pint		475 milliliters
32 oz	1 quart		950 milliliters
128 oz	1 gallon	3.75 liters	3750 milliliters

1/2 pound			252 grams
1.1 pounds			500 grams
2.2 pounds		1 kilo	1000 grams

1 lb flour	4 cups		
1 lb granulated sugar	2 cups		
1/4 lb butter	1/2 cup	1 stick	113.4 grams
1 lb butter	2 cups	4 sticks	453.6 grams

8 oz can	1 cup		226.8 grams
#1 can	1 1/4 cups		
#303 can	2 cups		453.6 grams

1 cup	1/2 pint	8 fluid ounces	237 ml
2 cups	1 pint	16 fluid ounces	474 ml
4 cups	1 quart	32 fluid ounces	948 ml
2 pints	1 quart	32 fluid ounces	948 ml
2 quarts	1/2 gallon	64 fluid ounces	1.896 liters
4 quarts	1 gallon	128 fluid ounces	3.792 liters

1 inch			0.0254 m
1 foot			0.3048 m

TEMPERATURES

DEGREES FAHRENHEIT	OVEN TEMPERATURE	DEGREES CELSIUS
250 – 300	very slow	121.11 – 148.89
300 – 325	slow	148.89 – 162.78
325 – 350	moderate	162.78 – 176.67
375	moderately hot	190.56
400 – 425	hot	204.44 – 218.33
450 +	very hot	232.22 +

NOTES